Understanding Love:™

Married for Life

Understanding Love:™

Married for Life

DR. MYLES MUNROE

Destiny Image® Publishers, Inc.
P.O. Box 310
Shippensburg, PA 17257-0310

"Speaking to the Purposes of God for This Generation
and for the Generations to Come"

Bahamas Faith Ministry
P.O. Box N9583
Nassau, Bahamas

ISBN 0-7684-2156-X

For Worldwide Distribution
Printed in the U.S.A.

This book and all other Destiny Image, Revival Press, MercyPlace,
Fresh Bread, Destiny Image Fiction, and Treasure House books are
available at Christian bookstores and distributors worldwide.

For a U.S. bookstore nearest you, call **1-800-722-6774**.
For more information on foreign distributors, call **717-532-3040**.
Or reach us on the Internet:
www.destinyimage.com

Dedication

To my beautiful, fantastic, awesome, wonderful, sensitive wife, Ruth; your support, respect, commitment, dedication, patience, and prayers for me make me look like a good husband and father. Thank you for making the principles in this book a practical reality. Thank you for making our marriage all I expected this adventure in human relations to be. I love you.

To my precious daughter, Charisa, and my beloved son, Chairo. May your marriages be built on the principles and precepts inherent in the distilled wisdom of the time tested truths of the Word of God. May this book become my greatest wedding gift to you and your children as you embrace its precepts.

To my father and late mother, Matthias and Louise Munroe. Your marriage of over 50 years became the living model and standard for me as I observed the beauty and benefit of a marriage built on the foundation of the word of God. Thank you for teaching me how to love my wife and children.

To all the unmarried singles who desire to have the successful marriage the Creator originally intended. May the wisdom of this book contribute to this desire.

To all married couples whose desire it is to improve and enhance their relationship. May you apply the principles of this book to assist in fulfilling your vows and to experience the marriage the creator originally intended for mankind.

To the source of all wisdom, knowledge and understanding, the Creator of the institute of marriage, my Lord and Redeemer, Jehovah Shalom, Yeshua.

Contents

CHAPTER ONE

Marriage: A Roleless Relationship

$\mathcal{M}$arriage is an adventure. I think most newlyweds would agree that the process of getting married is at once exciting, intimidating, and at least a little scary. After all, leaving the comfortable familiarity of one's childhood home and family to begin a new home and family with the man or woman of one's dreams is emotionally kin to pulling up stakes in one country and sailing across the ocean to start over in another. Getting married has a certain pioneer spirit about it—the flavor of the frontier. Everything is new and different, somewhat raw at first, with even a vague hint of danger.

In those heady days of courtship and engagement, wedding and honeymoon, the very air itself seems charged with magic and wonder. Full of life and vigor, the newlyweds feel ready to take on the world. No door is closed to them. No goal is too high, no dream too lofty. The world is their oyster. Nothing is beyond their grasp.

Eventually, however, reality sets in. The lustrous glow of the honeymoon fades somewhat, and the "we can conquer the world" attitude gives way to more down-to-earth pursuits. One day the couple awakens to the knowledge of a new truth. Looking each other in the face they realize, "Okay, we're married. *Now what?*" Now that they have pledged themselves to each other in a lifelong commitment, how do they make it work? How do they get from here to the hereafter while building a successful marriage along the way? What must they do to fulfill their dream of a lifelong relationship characterized by love, joy, friendship, and fruitfulness? How can they build a successful life together?

These are not idle questions. Success in marriage is not automatic. Likewise, being married does not guarantee either fellowship or communication. As a matter of fact, being married actually exposes how much a husband and wife *do not know* about each other. During courtship and engagement it is easy and customary for the man and woman to try to impress each other by showing only their best side—always looking right, dressing right, and acting right. It is after the wedding when their less attractive and less appealing qualities show themselves. When that happens, it can be quite a shock. Each person begins to see in the other things that he or she never dreamed existed.

One of the first challenges married couples face is reaching a mutual understanding of expectations and roles in the marriage. Failure to do so is one of the major causes of marital problems. Husbands and wives need to work out together the decision-making mechanics in the family and clearly articulate their expectations of each other. How will decisions be made and who will make them? What is the husband's "role"? What is the wife's "role"?

Most couples enter marriage with some preconceptions regarding roles. For example, the husband empties the garbage while the wife takes care of the dishes. The husband cares for the yard and the outside of the house while the wife does the laundry and the cooking and cleaning. The husband works to provide for his family while the wife manages the home and the children.

 Husbands and wives need to work out together the decision-making mechanics in the family and clearly articulate their expectations of each other.

Preconceptions of marital roles are not always correct. Why? One reason is that they are sometimes based on outdated customs or cultural ideas. Another reason is that they often fail to allow for individual gifts, talents, or abilities that are not necessarily gender-based. A successful marriage depends in part on a proper understanding of roles. Part of this understanding involves knowing the sources of common role perceptions and being able to evaluate the validity of those perceptions.

Sources of Common Role Perceptions in Marriage

Perceptions of marital roles, in western culture at least, generally arise from any of four common sources: tradition, parents, society, or the Church. Each of these sources exerts a powerful influence over the way husbands and wives view themselves and each other.

Tradition. Many of our most commonly held views of marital roles have been passed down to us through tradition. We adopt particular roles because "that's the way it has always been done." Husbands work at the office or factory as the family's "breadwinner"; wives work at home cooking, cleaning, and taking care of the children. Husbands rule over everything and everyone in the home, including their wives; wives submit passively to their husbands. Husbands make virtually all decisions affecting the family; wives go along with those decisions.

Tradition is not necessarily a bad thing. Sometimes tradition is important for maintaining stability and order. At the same time, however, we need to recognize that just because something is traditional does not mean that it is correct. Traditions can be founded on error just as easily as they can be founded on truth. Even if they were correct at one time, traditions have a way of outlasting the circumstances that originally brought them into being. Married couples must be very careful about defining roles based solely on tradition.

Traditions have a way of outlasting the circumstances that originally brought them into being.

Parents. Perhaps the most influential role perceptions in a marriage are those that the couple learns from their parents. Parents are, in fact, the primary channels through whom traditional role concepts are passed to the next generation. Most people adopt the role identities and relational methods they saw modeled at home while they were growing up. Whether those models were positive or negative, and despite their desire or intention to the contrary, most children grow up to be like their parents. One area where this is particularly true is in the raising and disciplining of children. Differing parenting philosophies and methods is a common point of conflict and disagreement for young married couples.

As with tradition, parental models of marital roles should be carefully evaluated because they may be wrong. Just because mom and dad did things a certain way for 40 or 50 years does not mean they did them right.

Society. Popular culture is another significant source for defining marital roles. This is distinct from tradition because where tradition remains unchanged for generations, social evolution is constantly creating new customs and trends. Modern society communicates its values and belief system primarily through the schools, through the entertainment industry (particularly television, movies, and popular music), and through the media. Throughout much of the western world these culture-shaping forces are dominated by a philosophy that is thoroughly rationalistic and humanistic in its worldview, allowing no place for either a Supreme Being or a truly spiritual dimension to life.

The pervasiveness of this influence makes it easy for anyone, even unwary believers, to easily pick up and internalize these values subconsciously. When believers bring worldly values and attitudes into their relationship, trouble always results. It is important that they keep their focus on the Word of God—the Bible—as their standard and source of knowledge.

> *When believers bring worldly values and attitudes into their relationship, trouble always results.*

Church. Traditionally, the Church has been one of the primary shapers of marital role perceptions in western culture. Although this is an appropriate function for the Church in society, it is an unfortunate fact that many of the "traditional" teachings of the Church regarding marital roles and male/female relationships in general have been negative, particularly where the woman is concerned.

For example, the Church in general has taught for many years that the woman is a "frail vessel," the "weaker sex," a fragile creature who must be handled with great care and not expected to perform any "heavy" tasks, either physical or mental. Modern research in biology and medicine has demonstrated conclusively that this is simply not true. Both physically and mentally, women are equal to men, although in different ways.

Another erroneous teaching is that women have little or nothing to offer spiritually to the overall life of a church. They are useful in service roles—the kitchen, the nursery, the choir—but not in *real* ministry like prophesying or laying hands on the sick.

The Church also has taught women to "submit" to their husbands no matter how they are treated. This is regarded as showing proper "respect" for their husbands. Wives who dare to strike back over harsh treatment are regarded as outcasts in the Church. Much of the traditional teaching on submission is based on a gross misunderstanding of the Scriptures, which has led to devastating results in the lives and relationships of countless women.

Much of the traditional teaching on submission is based on a gross misunderstanding of the Scriptures, which has led to devastating results in the lives and relationships of countless women.

Relating in Love

If the traditional sources for marital role perceptions are not always correct or relevant, what is to be done? Where can a married couple turn to find a reliable standard? Is there an "operating manual" for a successful marriage? Yes, there is. The best place to go for technical information on any product is the manufacturer. Marriage is no different. God created marriage and established it as the first and foremost of all human institutions and relationships. As the "manufacturer" of marriage, God understands it better than anyone else. It only makes sense, therefore, to refer to His "tech manual," the Bible, for information on how to make it work.

Surprisingly, many of the "traditional" marital roles are not specifically delineated in the Scriptures. There are no bulleted lists, no equations, and no formulas. What the Bible does provide are *principles*. Perhaps the most significant description of how husbands and wives are to relate to each other is found in the words of Paul, the first-century Jewish-Christian scholar, Church leader, and missionary:

Wives, submit to your husbands as to the Lord. For the husband is the head of the wife as Christ is the head of the church, His body, of which He is the Savior. Now as the church submits to Christ, so also wives should submit to their husbands in everything. Husbands, love your wives, just as Christ loved the church and gave Himself up for her to make her holy, cleansing her by the washing with water through the word, and to present her to Himself as a radiant church, without stain or wrinkle or any other blemish, but holy and blameless. In this same way, husbands ought to love their wives as their own bodies. He who loves his wife loves himself. After all, no one ever hated his own body, but he feeds and cares for it, just as Christ does the church—for we are members of His body. "For this reason a man will leave his father and mother and be united to his wife, and the two will become one flesh." This is a profound mystery—but I am talking about Christ and the church. However, each one of you also must love his wife as he loves himself, and the wife must respect her husband (Ephesians 5:22-33).

These verses mention nothing about specific, fixed "roles" for the husband and wife, but they do identify certain principles that should guide their relationship: submission, love, and respect. It is interesting to note that although Paul states four times that husbands should love their wives, he never once mentions that wives should love their husbands. Their love is implied in their submission to and respect for their husbands.

Clearly, Paul's emphasis here is on the attitude and behavior of the husbands: They are to love their wives "as Christ loved the church and gave Himself up for her." This focus on the husband is important for at least two reasons. First, by God's design the husband is the "head of the wife" and the spiritual leader of the home. His attitude and behavior will set the spiritual tone for the home and profoundly affect his wife's general and spiritual well-being.

The second reason is less evident to our modern-day social understanding. During the first century, when Paul wrote these words, women in both Jewish and Roman society were regarded as second-class citizens and had few rights of their own. Wives were viewed as little more than the property of their husbands. Paul's call for husbands to *love* their wives, particularly in the self-sacrificing way that Christ loved His Church, was a radically new concept, even revolutionary in its implications.

Love between a husband and wife was not itself new—ancient literature of every culture is full of love songs—but Paul's emphasis was. He was referring to a love in which a husband would serve his wife as Christ served the Church and would give his life for his wife as Christ gave His life for the Church. Sacrificial love is in itself a form of submission. Paul was talking about a love that would elevate a wife to *equal status* as a person in her husband's eyes.

 Sacrificial love is in itself a form of submission.

The closest this passage comes to defining marital roles is to say that a husband's "role" is to love his wife in a sacrificial, self-giving way, and a wife's "role" is to "submit" to her husband "as to the Lord" and to "respect" her husband. These "roles" are reciprocal. Any husband who is truly faithful to do *his* part will make it easy for his wife to do *her* part. Likewise, any wife who has a husband who loves her in this way will have no problem respecting him or submitting to his headship.

At the most basic level, then, a husband and wife should relate to each other through mutual love and submission rather than through a set of predefined roles, no matter what their source.

Relating without Roles

Essentially, marriage is a roleless relationship. It can be no other way if the marriage is truly grounded in sacrificial love. Sacrificial love is unconditional love—love without reason. True love has no reason; it just is. Unconditional love loves regardless of the behavior or "loveableness" of the ones loved, and whether or not they return that love. The New Testament identifies this kind of love with the Greek word *agape*. It is the kind of love that God exhibits toward a sinful human race, the kind of love that Jesus Christ demonstrated when He willingly died on the cross for that sinful race. As Paul wrote in his letter to the believers in Rome, "You see, at just the right time, when we were still powerless, Christ died for the ungodly. Very rarely will anyone die for a righteous man, though for a good man someone might possibly dare to die. But God demonstrates His own love for us in this: While we were still sinners, Christ died for us" (Rom. 5:6-8).

 Sacrificial love is unconditional love—love without reason.

God does not need a reason to love us; He loves us because love is His nature. His love for us does not hinge on whether or not we "turn over a new leaf," "clean up our act," or love Him in return. *Agape* makes no demands, holds no expectations, and carries no guarantees except to guarantee itself. The Lord guarantees that He will love us regardless of whether or not we return His love.

The love of Christ is a roleless love based on responses rather than expectations. His death on the cross was His love *responding* to humanity's need for forgiveness. Jesus placed no expectations on us as a pre-condition to His sacrifice. He gave His life freely with no guarantee that any of us would love Him back. The only expectation Jesus had was His own joy and exaltation before His Father: "Let us fix our eyes on Jesus, the author and perfecter of our faith, who for the joy set before Him endured the cross, scorning its shame, and sat down at the right hand of the throne of God" (Heb. 12:2).

His is an unconditional, open invitation: "For God so loved the world that He gave His one and only Son, that *whoever* believes in Him shall not perish but have eternal life" (Jn. 3:16, emphasis added); "Yet *to all who received Him*, to those who believed in His name, He gave the right to become children of God" (Jn. 1:12, emphasis added). These words imply that Jesus had no guarantee. His love led Him to the cross, and He still would have died even if no one had believed in Him or received Him. *Agape* has no reason.

Love that looks for a reason is love with conditions attached. Conditions give rise to expectations. By expectations I mean those mundane and routine jobs, functions, or activities that husbands and wives automatically expect each other to do because it is their "role," such as washing the dishes, cooking the meals, cleaning the house, cutting the grass, making the bed, bathing the children, and so on. Expectations lead inevitably to disappointment. Disappointment leads to arguments, which strain the relationship, which then endangers fellowship.

What does all this have to do with a roleless relationship in marriage? Marital love is supposed to be like the love that Jesus has for His Church: unconditional, sacrificial, and without expectations or guarantees. Fixed roles create expectations, and expectations imply guarantees. For example, if a wife sees mowing the lawn as her husband's "role," that role creates in her mind the expectation that he will cut the grass when it gets tall. If he does not, he has violated the "guarantee." Her expectation turns to disappointment or even anger, and conflict results. If a husband believes that meal preparation is his wife's "role," he will be upset if supper is not on the table when he gets home from work. His wife has not fulfilled the "guarantee" implied in his expectation, which is based on his perception of her "role."

Fixed roles create expectations, and expectations imply guarantees.

The upshot of all this is that love without reasons is love without expectations. If there are no expectations, there are no fixed roles. Marriage then becomes a relationship based on responding to needs rather than adhering to rigid preconceptions. If a husband and wife have no rigid role expectations of each other, neither will be disappointed. A response-based approach to marriage will bring a deep, fresh, and new dimension to the relationship. Married couples will experience greater success and happiness the more they learn how to relate without fixed roles.

Temporary Responsibilities, Not Permanent Roles

A roleless relationship in a marriage does not mean that nobody does anything or that the couple takes a random or haphazard approach to their home life. On the contrary, it is important for a husband and wife to come to a clear and mutual understanding of how things will be done. A relationship without fixed roles *does* mean that each partner will respond according to need, ability, and opportunity. Who regularly cooks the meals? That may depend on who is the better cook. Some husbands can cook better than their wives can. In that case, why should the wife be saddled with the responsibility to prepare the meals simply because that is her "traditional" role?

A role is a temporary responsibility that is based on the ability of the one who responds. As such, roles can change from one day to the next, from one minute to the next, and from one person to the other depending on the need of the moment. What needs to be done? Who can do it the best? Who is in the best position to do it right now? It is a matter of need, ability, and opportunity. That's why it would probably be better to refer to marital tasks as responsibilities rather than roles.

Whatever the need, whoever is able and available at the time is responsible.

Relating without fixed roles is a natural outgrowth of a marriage based on *agape* and in which the husband and wife truly are equal partners. *Agape* seeks to serve rather than to be served. Jesus demonstrated this principle in a powerful example recorded in John 13:3-17. On the night before He was crucified, Jesus gathered with His followers to celebrate the Passover. As the disciples entered, no one was present to wash their feet (a task normally assigned to the most menial of servants) and none of them volunteered to do it. Their unspoken attitude was, "That's not my job!" Jesus Himself got up from the table, took off His outer clothing, wrapped a towel around His waist as a servant would, and proceeded to wash His disciples' feet. There was no question of roles. Jesus saw a need and responded to it. At the same time, He taught His followers a valuable lesson in humility and service.

Agape expresses itself in conscious response to recognized needs. It is not an automatic or unconscious reaction to stimuli based on conditioned habits or attitudes. A husband's anger at his wife's "failure" to wash the clothes may be simply a conditioned reaction to her violation of his role concept for her. An *agape* response would be to think before acting or speaking and evaluate the situation to see if there are mitigating circumstances—a legitimate reason why the laundry has not been done. Perhaps she has been caught up all day caring for a sick child. She may be under tremendous stress on the job or up to her eyebrows in homework for her night class. Whatever the reason, *agape* seeks to help with a need, not criticize a failure. Even if this husband and wife have a mutual understanding that she will normally take care of the laundry, in this instance the *agape* response—the roleless response—may be for him to wash the clothes and take some of the load off her. *Agape* doesn't look for roles; *agape* responds to needs.

AGAPE *expresses itself in conscious response to recognized needs.*

Husbands and wives who approach their marriage from a roleless perspective assume full ownership of every aspect of their life together. There are no "his" and "her" roles, only "our" responsibilities. Who does what, and when, depends on the specific circumstances. Each couple should arrive at a mutual agreement as to which of them has the *primary* responsibility for each task or need, understanding as well that ultimately they share all responsibilities together.

Assignment of marital responsibilities may depend on each person's training, abilities, or temperament. Who should prepare the meals (primarily)? Whoever is the best cook. Who should manage the family finances (primarily)? Whoever has the best head for figures and bookkeeping. Who should do the house cleaning? Whoever lives in the house. Who should wash the dishes? Whoever dirties them. Who should make the bed? Whoever sleeps in it. Who should mow the lawn? Whoever has the time and the opportunity.

Clear assignment of primary authority and responsibility between a husband and wife establishes order and helps prevent chaos and confusion. At the same time, rather than producing rigidity in the relationship, it allows for flexibility so that either partner can do what is needed at any given time. Whoever can, does; whoever sees, acts. It's that simple.

Functioning in marital responsibilities also will be affected by whether or not both partners have jobs outside the home. A stay-at-home wife can reasonably be expected to regularly bear a larger share of the domestic responsibilities than can a wife who works a full-time job. Sharing responsibilities becomes even more important when both the husband and wife are away from home during the day. Each partner needs to take into account the schedule and obligations of the other,

including those of work. Mutual understanding and coopera-
tion are essential.

 Whoever can, does; whoever sees, acts. It's that simple.

So then, what is the husband's "role" in the marriage? He
is the "head" of the home, the spiritual leader responsible for
the spiritual direction of the family. He is to love his wife in
the same way that Christ loved the Church, sacrificially and
unconditionally. What is the wife's "role"? She is to respect
her husband and submit to his headship. In the practical matters of home life they both should respond according to the
need, their abilities, and their availability.

PRINCIPLES

1. At the most basic level, a husband and wife should relate to each other through mutual love and sub-mission rather than through a set of predefined roles.

2. Essentially, marriage is a roleless relationship.

3. The love of Christ is a roleless love based on re-sponses rather than expectations.

4. If there are no expectations, there are no fixed roles. Marriage then becomes a relationship based on re-sponding to needs rather than adhering to rigid preconceptions.

5. A relationship without fixed roles *does* mean that each partner will respond according to need, ability, and opportunity.

6. A role is a temporary responsibility that is based on the ability of the one who responds.

7. *Agape* doesn't look for roles; *agape* responds to needs.

8. In a roleless marriage there are no "his" and "her" roles, only "our" responsibilities.

9. Assignment of marital responsibilities may depend on each person's training, abilities, or temperament.

CHAPTER TWO

The Question of Submission

*L*earning how to relate without fixed roles can be a major challenge for married couples, particularly if traditional role concepts are deeply ingrained in their minds. Successfully making the change will require significant adjustments in their thinking. Because most human cultures have operated for so long under the paradigm of a male-dominated social order, the concept of marriage as a partnership of equals characterized by a roleless relationship does not come easily to many people. Nevertheless, that is the biblical model.

In the beginning, God created man—male and female—in His own image and gave *them* dominion over the earth to rule it *together* (see Gen. 1:26). The first human couple enjoyed a marriage in which they were equal partners, sharing equal rights and equal responsibilities. They walked in open and continual fellowship with each other and with God.

The day came when Adam and Eve chose to disobey God. Immediately their circumstances changed. Their sin broke their fellowship with God and caused their equal-partnership marriage to degenerate into a shadow of its former self with the woman subjugated to her husband. This corrupted, male-dominated marriage became the "normal" pattern for male/female relationships in a sin-tainted world.

From the start God had a plan to restore mankind to fellowship with Himself. He sent His Son, Jesus Christ, to die on a cross for the sins of humanity, thereby breaking the power of sin and destroying its effects. Part of God's plan was to restore the institution of marriage to its original, pristine condition.

 The first human couple enjoyed a marriage in which they were equal partners, sharing equal rights and equal responsibilities. They walked in open and continual fellowship with each other and with God.

A marriage between believers can and should be characterized by a roleless relationship in which both the husband and wife are equal partners. This, however, raises the natural question of how to reconcile the biblical concept of equal partnership in marriage with the equally biblical concept of a wife being in submission to her husband. On the surface these appear to be opposite and irreconcilable ideas. In the previous chapter we touched briefly on this subject, but understanding the question of submission is so critical to long-term success and happiness in marriage that we need to take a much closer look at it.

Husbands Should Act Like Jesus

We already have seen that mutual love, submission, and respect should characterize husband/wife relations in a biblical marriage, but what exactly does this mean? Consider once again the counsel that Paul gave to the Ephesians:

Submit to one another out of reverence for Christ. Wives, submit to your husbands as to the Lord. For the husband is the head of the wife as Christ is the head of the church, His body, of which He is the Savior. Now as the church submits to Christ, so also wives should submit to their husbands in everything. Husbands, love your wives, just as Christ loved the church and gave Himself up for her to make her holy, cleansing her by the washing with water through the word, and to present her to Himself as a radiant church, without stain or wrinkle or any other blemish, but holy and blame-less. In this same way, husbands ought to love their wives as their own bodies. He who loves his wife loves himself. After all, no one ever hated his own body, but he feeds and cares for it, just as Christ does the church—for we are members of His body. "For this reason a man will leave his father and moth-er and be united to his wife, and the two will become one flesh." This is a profound mystery—but I am talking about Christ and the church. However, each one of you also must love his wife as he loves himself, and the wife must respect her husband (Ephesians 5:21-33).

Paul's first instruction concerns mutual submission: "Sub-mit to *one another* out of reverence for Christ." Everything Paul says in these verses is in the context of mutual submission. A wife submits to her husband "as to the Lord" and the husband loves his wife "just as Christ loved the church and gave Him-self up for her." This self-giving love on the part of the hus-band is itself a form of submission. It is this submission by the husband on behalf of his wife that is so often overlooked in teaching and in practice.

Throughout this passage Paul compares the husband to Christ. Wives are to respect and submit to their husbands "as to the Lord." The husband is "the head of the wife as Christ is the head of the church." Husbands are to love their wives "just as Christ loved the church and gave Himself up for her." In every case, the husband is to look to Christ as the example for his own behavior. What this means in practical terms is that a husband deserves and has the right to expect submission and respect from his wife to the extent and degree that he lives and acts like Jesus toward her. A husband deserves his wife's sub-mission as long as he acts like the Lord. If he does not act like the Lord, then he has no right to expect his wife to submit to him "as to the Lord."

A husband deserves his wife's submission as long as he acts like the Lord.

Paul says that wives are to submit to their husbands "as the church submits to Christ." How does Jesus get His Church to submit to Him? What would happen if Jesus suddenly appeared and walked through your church swinging a baseball bat to see how many heads He could knock off, and yelling, "Listen up! You'd better do what I say, or else!" What if He started cursing His Church or kicking and spitting and bad-mouthing His Church? There would be an epidemic of backsliding, and I would be one of them. He would lose followers left and right. Who would want to follow that kind of "loving" Lord?

No, Jesus won the love, respect, and submission of His Church through His own submission to her in sacrificial love. Freely and willingly He gave His life for the Church. With His blood He cleansed the Church of sin and guilt and made her holy, blameless, and without any stain or blemish. Through His Spirit Jesus strengthens and sustains the Church, always loving her and showing compassion to her, always forgiving her, and always providing for her needs according to His riches in glory (see Phil. 4:19).

Jesus is the perfect example. If husbands want to learn how to win their wives' love, respect, and submission, they need to look at how Jesus treats His Church and follow His pattern.

 If husbands want to learn how to win their wives' love, respect, and submission, they need to look at how Jesus treats His Church and follow His pattern.

Most Husbands Have Dropped the Ball

Unfortunately, the sad truth is that, measured against the standard set by Jesus, most husbands don't deserve submission.

When it comes to loving their wives the way Christ loved the Church, most husbands have dropped the ball. This does not mean that the majority of husbands do not sincerely love their wives and want to do their best by them. The failure of husbands to measure up to Christ's standard reveals a fundamental flaw that lies at the heart of every man, a flaw shared also by every woman. The Bible calls this flaw "sin," and it has been a part of human nature ever since the first human couple defied God in the Garden of Eden and went their own way. Sin is the flaw that prevents husbands from measuring up to Jesus' example.

 Measured against the standard set by Jesus, most husbands don't deserve submission.

Although Adam and Eve enjoyed equal partnership and authority in the Garden of Eden, God had appointed Adam as the "head" of the family with the overall responsibility of teaching and guiding his wife in the ways of God. After Adam and Eve disobeyed God, sin became part of their nature. It destroyed their fellowship with God and made them fearful of Him so that they hid themselves. When God came looking for them, He sought out Adam first. Even though Eve was the first to disobey and then drew her husband in, Adam was the "head," and God held him primarily responsible.

> But the Lord God called to the man, "Where are you?" He answered, "I heard You in the garden, and I was afraid because I was naked; so I hid." And He said, "Who told you that you were naked? Have you eaten from the tree that I commanded you not to eat from?" The man said, "The woman You put here with me—she gave me some fruit from the tree, and I ate it" (Genesis 3:9-12).

As soon as he was confronted with his failure, Adam tried to shift the blame to his wife. Refusing to acknowledge his guilt, Adam tried to transfer responsibility to someone else—and men have been transferring responsibility for their failures ever since.

When Adam disobeyed God and sin entered his nature, four things happened immediately in his life. First, he knew he was guilty. He refused to acknowledge it, but he knew it. Second, he became afraid. Sin caused separation between man and God and that separation created fear. Third, he hid himself, and, fourth, he felt shame.

> *Refusing to acknowledge his guilt, Adam tried to transfer responsibility to someone else—and men have been transferring responsibility for their failures ever since.*

All of these are the common experience of all men. Even today men know when they are wrong even if they never admit it. The thought of being exposed as a failure fills them with fear. Men still hide from their failures. Many hide behind their ego, their physical strength, or their position or status in the community. Others hide behind money, influence, political power, their jobs, sports—anything that helps them avoid having to deal with their failures.

Although few would readily admit it, when a man messes up he feels ashamed, no matter how tough he might act. He may disguise his shame with bragging talk or "macho" behavior with the "boys." He may try to drown it in liquor or act out his self-hatred by beating his wife and kids. The shame of a failed marriage may drive him into the arms of a mistress. He may seek to deflect his shame by blaming his wife for his failures.

Nothing destroys a man's ego like failure. Men have a great fear of being "naked"—of having their failure exposed for all the world to see. That's why so many men seek out false security in persons or environments that will affirm their manhood without bringing up their shortcomings. They would rather bask in the warmth of a false self-image than face the truth about themselves.

Husbands Should Shoulder Their Responsibilities

So here is the dilemma: Husbands are supposed to act like Jesus, yet few husbands do. Of course, no one is perfect; no husband can perfectly model the behavior of Christ. The problem is that so many husbands really have no clue how they are supposed to act or what they are supposed to do. They have been hiding from their true selves for so long that even if they realize that they need to change, they don't know how.

Husbands who are serious about following Jesus' example in relating to their wives must be willing to shoulder their responsibilities. They must be willing to accept responsibility for their actions without denying them, hiding from them, or shifting the blame to someone else, particularly their wives. They need to recognize that because they are human they will occasionally fail, but this does not have to be a cause of shame or disaster. A relationship established on *agape* will create an environment of forgiveness and support. Any husband who honestly tries to love his wife "as Christ loved the church" will find her at his side ready and eager to help him succeed. What reasonable woman could fail to respond to a man who truly loves her, covers her, protects her, provides for her, gives himself for her, and, humanly speaking, makes her the center of his world?

Within the overall context of loving his wife, a husband's first and primary role is to be the spiritual head and covering and teacher in the home. Through his words, lifestyle, and personal behavior the husband should teach the Word, the will, and the ways of the Lord to his wife and children.

One of the biggest problems in marriage and family life today is that in so many homes the husband has effectively abdicated his headship either by default or ignorance. In many believing households the wife knows more about the Lord and His Word and ways than her husband does because she spends more time exposed to them. She is in church while her husband is off somewhere else doing his own thing. Even if he is in church with her, the husband frequently is less engaged and involved in spiritual matters than his wife is. How can a husband teach what he does not know? How can he model for his family a lifestyle he knows nothing about?

 One of the biggest problems in marriage and family life today is that in so many homes the husband has effectively abdicated his headship either by default or ignorance.

If more husbands were faithful in loving their wives as Christ loved the Church and in fulfilling their responsibility as head of the home, there would be little problem or confusion over the issue of wives being in submission.

Husbands Should Woo their Wives as Christ Wooed the Church

Just as Paul compares the husband to Christ, he compares the wife to the Church. Wives are to submit to their husbands as the Church submits to Christ. At the same time, husbands are to love their wives as Christ loved the Church. The two are reciprocal actions: As the husband loves his wife sacrificially, his wife submits to him.

Husbands must win their wives' submission by making themselves worthy of it. They do this by learning to love their wives in the way that Christ loves His Church. How does Christ love His Church? How does He draw His people to Him so that they submit to Him?

The two are reciprocal actions: As the husband loves his wife sacrificially, his wife submits to him.

Jesus wins us by wooing us. First He reveals Himself to us in some way and captures our heart with His love. Then He gently draws us to Himself: "I have loved you with an everlasting love; I have drawn you with loving-kindness" (Jer. 31:3b). He extends an open invitation for us to come to Him, be forgiven of our sins, and receive the gift of everlasting life. Once we understand how much He loves us and how much He has done for us, we realize that we would be crazy *not* to follow Him. That's when, in response to His gentle drawing, we decide *of our own free will* to come to Him.

Submitting ourselves to Christ is *our* choice. He never pushes His way in. Jesus never twists our arm or pressures us in any other way. He simply says, "Here I am. Come to Me." Submission is never forced from without. Submission is freely chosen and willingly given. Once we submit ourselves to Jesus, He becomes the center of our life. He has wooed us so well and we love Him so much that we are ready to go anywhere and do anything for Him.

In the same way, a husband should woo his wife. Always hold her in highest honor and regard her with utmost respect as a person. Cover her with prayer and protect her. Treat her with kindness, consideration, and compassion. Don't be afraid to show tender affection. Remember to do little acts of thoughtfulness. Buy her flowers. Take her to dinner at a fine restaurant. Surprise her with a weekend getaway just for two. In words, in deeds, and in every other way possible, let her know that she is loved, valued, and regarded above all others.

A Wife's Submission Is Voluntary

So far we have focused almost exclusively on the responsibilities of the husband. This is for at least two reasons: first, because the husband bears the greater responsibility since he is the head of the home, and second, because his responsibility is so widely misunderstood and therefore so rarely fulfilled.

The husband is the "head" of his wife; he is not her "boss." Neither is he the "boss" of the home. This is where so many husbands misunderstand. It may be a narrow distinction, but Christ *leads* His Church, He does not *rule* His Church, as with a heavy iron fist. Christ rules His Kingdom, but He *leads* His Church. He loves and cherishes His Church, and His Church submits to Him freely and willingly.

So what about the wife? What is her responsibility with regard to her husband? Consider again Paul's instructions in Ephesians: "Wives, submit to your husbands as to the Lord.... Now as the church submits to Christ, so also wives should submit to their husbands in everything" (Eph. 5:22,24). How does the Church submit to Christ, its Lord? Freely and willingly, out of love. Those qualities should also characterize a wife's submission to her husband.

Paul's words in these verses constitute a command: "Wives, submit to your husbands." Notice that this command is given to the wives, not to the husbands. Wives are commanded to submit to their husbands. Nowhere does Paul either command or give any authority to husbands to force their wives to submit. Forced submission is not true submission; it is subjugation. Submission is always freely chosen and willingly given.

Even though submission is commanded for the wife, her compliance is *voluntary*. She has the right to choose. As far as her husband is fulfilling his responsibility and seeking to love her with the same kind of sacrificial, self-giving love with which Christ loved the Church, a wife has the responsibility to submit to him "in everything." If she fails to do so, she is accountable not so much to her husband as to the Lord. Her failure to be in submission to her husband's headship is sin.

Forced submission is not true submission; it is subjugation.

A wife's submission to a godly husband who strives to be like Jesus in his attitude and behavior toward her is not a demeaning or demoralizing act. Submission does not mean humiliation or abject subjection of a wife's personality and will to the whim and will of her husband. A husband who acts like Jesus toward his wife will not subject her to this kind of treatment anyway.

Submission means that a wife acknowledges her husband's headship as spiritual leader and guide for the family. It has nothing whatsoever to do with her denying or suppressing her will, her spirit, her intellect, her gifts, or her personality. To submit means to recognize, affirm, and support her husband's God-given responsibility of overall family leadership. Biblical submission of a wife to her husband is a submission of *position*, not personhood. It is the free and willing subordination of an *equal* to an *equal* for the sake of order, stability, and obedience to God's design.

As a man, a husband will fulfill his destiny and his manhood as he exercises his headship in prayerful and humble submission to Christ and gives himself in sacrificial love to his wife. As a woman, a wife will realize her womanhood as she submits to her husband in honor of the Lord, receiving his love and accepting his leadership. When a proper relationship of mutual submission is present and active, a wife will be released and empowered to become the woman God always intended her to be.

Proper understanding and exercise of biblical submission by *both* the husband and wife are critical to the long-term success and happiness of any marriage. Without them, the couple will never realize their complete identity in Christ or release their full potential as human beings created in God's image.

PRINCIPLES

@

1. A husband deserves and has the right to expect submission and respect from his wife to the extent and degree that he lives and acts like Jesus toward her.

2. Sin is the flaw that prevents husbands from measuring up to Jesus' example.

3. Within the overall context of loving his wife, a husband's first and primary role is to be the spiritual head and covering and teacher in the home.

4. Husbands must win their wives' submission by making themselves worthy of it. They do this by learning to love their wives in the way that Christ loves His Church.

5. Submission is never forced from without. Submission is freely chosen and willingly given.

6. As far as her husband is fulfilling his responsibility and seeking to love her with the same kind of sacrificial, self-giving love with which Christ loved the Church, a wife has the responsibility to submit to him "in everything."

7. Biblical submission of a wife to her husband is a submission of *position*, not personhood. It is the free and willing subordination of an *equal* to an *equal* for the sake of order, stability, and obedience to God's design.

CHAPTER THREE

Mastering the Art of Communication

*A*mong the complaints that marriage counselors hear most frequently are statements like, "She just doesn't understand me," or "He never listens to me." The vast majority of marriages that are on the rocks today have run aground, either directly or indirectly, because of the couple's inability to communicate with each other.

Over my many years in ministry I have counseled hundreds of couples with marital problems. In all but a handful of cases the troubled relationship stemmed essentially from a communication breakdown at its core. Whenever I counsel a married couple, several ground rules apply. First, when the husband talks, the wife listens. Second, when the wife talks, the husband listens. Third, after both of them have talked, I talk and they listen. While one is speaking, no one else interrupts. It is always interesting to see the look of astonishment that so often appears on the face of each spouse while the other one is speaking. In many cases, this is the first time in months or even years that they have actually *listened* to each other, and they are absolutely amazed at what they hear.

Communication is an art that must be learned, a skill that must be mastered. It does not happen automatically, even in marriage. True communication can occur only in an environment conducive to honest self-expression. Many couples spend a lot of time talking *at* each other but very little time actually talking *to* each other. Just because they are talking does not mean they are communicating.

The only time some couples talk is when they argue. Sometimes critical statements and negative comments are virtually all a husband and wife hear from each other. Communication is best learned in an open, honest, and non-confrontational environment. Couples who do not learn how to communicate in such a low-key setting will never be able to do it in a confrontational situation.

Building the environment for effective communication must be deliberately planned. If I want to grow a nice garden, I cannot leave it to chance. I have to choose a spot for maximum sunlight, prepare the soil, plant the seeds, add fertilizer, pull weeds regularly, and make sure the plants get adequate water. In the same way, an environment conducive to communication must be built and nurtured deliberately and with great care. Couples who establish and maintain an atmosphere of openness, trust, and grace for talking about the good things also will find it much easier to talk about tough issues when they arise.

 Communication is best learned in an open, honest, and non-confrontational environment.

Communication is to love what blood is to life. Leviticus 17:11 says that life is in the blood. It is impossible to have any kind of healthy relationship without communication. This is true for anyone, whether regarding human relationships or a relationship with God.

Understanding Communication

Part of the problem with communication in marriage stems from the fact that many couples are confused about what it really means to communicate. Genuine communication requires both speaking and understanding. "Speaking" refers to any means by which thoughts, ideas, or feelings are expressed, whether by voice, gestures, body language, or facial expressions. Understanding involves not only hearing what was said, but also interpreting what was said according to the speaker's intention.

Communication between male and female or husband and wife is complicated by the fact that men and women think differently, perceive things differently, and respond differently. In general, men are logical thinkers and women are emotional feelers. Men speak what they are thinking while women speak what they are feeling. Men interpret what they hear from a logical frame of reference and women, from an emotional frame of reference. In other words, a man and a woman can hear the exact same message at the exact same time from the exact same speaker and perceive that message in two completely different ways. The same problem can easily arise when they are trying to communicate with each other.

Many people seem to equate conversation with communication. Just because two people talk to each other does not necessarily mean that they understand each other. What one says may not be what the other one hears, and what one hears may not be what the other one means. Two-way conversation does not guarantee communication. Once again, the key is understanding.

Understanding goes beyond simple acknowledgement of someone's spoken word. The verbal element is only a small part of the overall dynamic of human communication. Nonverbal elements such as gestures, facial expressions, and body language play an even greater part than the spoken word in determining how we interpret the messages we receive. Which would you believe, if I said, "I love you," with a warm smile, or through gritted teeth with a scowl on my face and fist clinched? Although the words are the same, the message conveyed is totally different.

Non-verbal elements such as gestures, facial expressions, and body language play an even greater part than the spoken word in determining how we interpret the messages we receive.

Communication is a process by which information is exchanged between individuals or groups utilizing a common system of symbols, signs, or behavior. To communicate is to transmit information, thought, or feeling so that it is satisfactorily received or understood. It is a two-way interaction between people in which messages are both sent and received and where both parties understand what the other party means. If I speak to you and you speak back to me, confirming with me that what you heard and understood me to say is what I really meant, then true communication has taken place.

If the key to communication is understanding, the key to understanding is listening.

Listen Up!

In our fast-paced, high-stress modern society today, listening has become almost a lost art. Failure to listen is one of the most frequent problems related to communication. So often our natural tendency is to speak before we listen. We could avoid a lot of hurt, misunderstanding, and embarassment if we would simply learn to listen before we speak.

Epictetus, a first-century Greek philosopher, said, "We have two ears and one mouth so that we can listen twice as much as we speak." There is a great deal of truth in that statement. The Bible contains many similar words of wisdom. Throughout the Scriptures, listening is linked to knowledge and understanding. Over and over the Book of Proverbs calls us to *listen* to words of wisdom and learn. Time and again Jesus appealed to the crowds to *listen* to Him: "Jesus called the crowd to Him and said, 'Listen and understand'" (Mt. 15:10).

Many are the times when Jesus said, "He who has ears, let him hear."

Perhaps the most direct reference to the balance between listening and speaking is found in the New Testament Book of James: "My dear brothers, take note of this: Everyone should be quick to listen, slow to speak and slow to become angry, for man's anger does not bring about the righteous life that God desires" (Jas. 1:19-20). James links the readiness to listen with the ability to avoid uninformed speech and unnecessary or inappropriate anger. How many times do married couples spout off and get angry with each other simply because they do not take the time to listen first? We could paraphrase James' counsel this way: "Listen first! Don't be in a hurry to talk, and even then be careful what you say and how you say it. Don't have a short fuse because explosive anger will only sabotage your spiritual growth."

Listening involves more than simply hearing or comprehending what someone says. Everything we hear passes through the filters of our own beliefs and experiences as well as our knowledge and impression of the speaker. These filters color how we interpret what we hear and can cause us sometimes to misunderstand the speaker's meaning. Good listening involves reaching beyond our filters to hear what other people are really saying, not only with their words, but also with their tone of voice, their facial expressions, and their body language.

Another problem related to listening is when we are more concerned about our own words than we are with the other person's words. Have you ever been talking to someone and found that rather than listening to them you are busy thinking about what you are going to say next? Have you ever felt that someone else was not listening to you for the same reason? This kind of thing happens all the time and we call it "conversation." It may be conversation, but it is not communication because no one is listening. There is no exchange of information with confirmed mutual understanding.

Part of the art of listening is learning to give the other person our full attention, taking a genuine interest in what he or she has to say with an honest desire to understand. If communication is our goal, we need to focus more on the other person's words, ideas, and values than on our own. Nothing in the world blesses a person like having someone listen—*really listen*—to him or her.

Nothing in the world blesses a person like having someone listen—really listen—to him or her.

Proper and effective listening requires that we get our full faculties involved. In order for genuine communication to take place, we must learn to listen *fully*, engaging body, mind, intellect, emotions, eyes, ears—in short, everything. We need to listen *first* and set aside our own thoughts and words and agenda long enough to hear and understand the other person. Once we understand and the other person knows that we understand, then we can respond more appropriately from the context of that understanding. This establishes a clear channel for genuine two-way communication to take place.

Holistic Communication

Because communication is an art, it must be deliberately, patiently, and carefully learned over time. Effective face-to-face communication is always holistic in nature, involving all the senses and the full engagement of body, intellect, and mental energy.

Communication is an exchange of information—a message—between individuals in such a way as to bring mutual understanding. Every message contains three essential components: content, tone of voice, and nonverbal signals such as gestures, facial expressions, and body language. When all three work in harmony, the probability of mutual understanding is very high. If any element is missing or contrary to the others, the likelihood of successful communication diminishes significantly.

In any communication where human emotions and personalities are involved, nonverbal elements are more significant than verbal. This is easily verified in life. A friend has just lost a loved one. You want to help, to express sympathy, but you don't know what to say. Quite often in a situation like this words are totally inadequate. Of greater value to your friend is simply your physical presence. A hug, a warm embrace, sharing quiet tears together—these simple nonverbal acts communicate your love and support for your friend much more clearly than could any number of fumbling words, no matter how well-intentioned they might be.

Research bears this out as well. Studies in communication have shown that the verbal aspect—the basic content—comprises only 7 percent of the total message that we send or that another person receives. Tone of voice accounts for 38 percent while the remaining 55 percent is nonverbal. In other words, how someone else perceives and understands us depends only 7 percent on *what* we say, 38 percent on *how* we say it, and 55 percent on what we are *doing* when we say it.

If we wish to avoid misunderstanding, hurt feelings, and arguments, we need to be careful to make sure that our tone of voice and our gestures, facial expressions, and body language send the same message as the words we speak with our lips.

This area of the nonverbal is where so many people—and so many married couples—have so much difficulty in communication. Problems arise between a husband and wife when there is a disconnection between *what* they say to each other and *how* they say it. The wrong tone of voice can be particularly devastating, causing an otherwise simple disagreement or misunderstanding to escalate into a shouting match or a hurtful barrage of sarcastic barbs fired back and forth.

 Problems arise between a husband and wife when there is a disconnection between what they say to each other and how they say it.

For this reason, it would be good for couples to remember James' counsel to "be quick to listen, slow to speak and slow to become angry." Proverbs 15:1 provides another valuable bit of advice: "A gentle answer turns away wrath, but a harsh word stirs up anger." When trying to communicate with each other, a husband and wife should be careful to make sure their voices and faces agree with their words.

Five Levels of Communication

Most relationships never get beyond superficial interaction. Lasting relationships, however, move deeper. One sign of a healthy and growing relationship is a deepening level of intimacy in the interaction and communication of those involved in the relationship.

People interact for the most part at one or more of five different levels of communication, each level being deeper and more intimate than the previous one. At the lowest level is casual conversation. It is superficial and safe, such as the kind of talk we would have with a stranger in line with us at the supermarket. "Hello, how are you?" "I'm fine, and you?" "I'm fine, too. How are the children?" "They're fine. What do you think about this weather we're having?" There are no deep probing questions and no painful or embarrassing personal revelations, only polite, courteous, and inconsequential conversation. Everything is non-threatening and non-committal.

The next highest level of communication involves reporting the facts about others. This is the kind of conversation in which we are content to talk with others about what someone else has said or done, but offer no personal information or opinions on these things. This is the level of the objective journalist, reporting only the facts of a situation, and then usually only what someone else has said. It involves no personal element.

Level three is where true communication first occurs because we begin to express our ideas, opinions, or decisions with the specific intention of being heard and understood by others. This openness also places us for the first time at a level of personal risk. Anytime we reveal any part of our inner selves—thoughts, ideas, beliefs, opinions—we open the door to possible rejection or ridicule. Intimacy is growing at this level, but there is still a safety zone. Our personal beliefs and ideas are less vulnerable to injury than are our emotions and innermost being, which at this level are still safely tucked away.

At level four we feel secure and intimate enough to begin sharing our emotions. Although deep and serious communication occurs at this level, there is still a guarded quality to the relationship. We are not yet ready to open up completely and let the other person see us as we really are deep down inside.

The highest level of all is the level of complete emotional and personal communication, characterized by absolute openness and honesty. At this level there are no secrets and no "off-limits" areas. We are ready and willing to lay our hearts bare, to open up every room and every compartment and invite close inspection. There is no greater or deeper level of intimacy than when two people feel free and secure enough to be completely honest with each other. At the same time, the risks of rejection or ridicule are at their greatest as well. Risk is unavoidable where true intimacy is involved. One way to define intimacy is the willingness and trust to make oneself completely open and vulnerable to another. Vulnerability always involves risk, but there is no other path to true intimacy or genuine communication at its deepest level.

 Risk is unavoidable where true intimacy is involved.

Long-term success and fulfillment in marriage depends to a large degree on the scope and depth to which a husband and wife develop their art of communication. It is vitally important that they learn how to listen to and understand one another and feel comfortable sharing their deepest and innermost thoughts, feelings, joys, sorrows, hopes, and dreams. Marriage is a lifelong journey of adventure with surprises and challenges at every turn. Learning to communicate effectively is also the journey of a lifetime. It is neither quick nor easy, but it yields increasing rewards of intimacy and fulfillment through the years that are well worth the hard work required.

PRINCIPLES

1. True communication can occur only in an environment conducive to honest self-expression.

2. Genuine communication requires both speaking and understanding.

3. To communicate is to transmit information, thought, or feeling so that it is satisfactorily received or understood.

4. The key to communication is understanding, and the key to understanding is listening.

5. Good listening involves reaching beyond our filters to hear what other people are really saying, not only with their words, but also with their tone of voice, their facial expressions, and their body language.

6. Effective face-to-face communication is always holistic in nature, involving all the senses and the full engagement of body, intellect, and mental energy.

7. How someone else perceives and understands us depends only 7 percent on *what* we say, 38 percent on *how* we say it, and 55 percent on what we are *doing* when we say it.

8. One sign of a healthy and growing relationship is a deepening level of intimacy in the interaction and communication of those involved in the relationship.

9. One way to define intimacy is the willingness and trust to make oneself completely open and vulnerable to another.

CHAPTER FOUR

Don't Forget the Little Things

*U*nderstanding and practicing general concepts such as marital responsibilities, submission, and communication are key to a happy and successful marriage. As critical as these principles are, however, ultimate success depends also in giving attention to the "little things"—those simple, ongoing, daily courtesies and considerations that enhance communication and add sweetness to a relationship. Because they are simple, the "little things" can be easily overlooked amidst the clamor of more pressing concerns.

In marriage, as in any other endeavor, we cannot afford to underestimate the importance of "little things" to overall success. The Great Wall of China was built one brick at a time. The Great Pyramid on the Giza plateau in Egypt rose up stone by stone. Ignoring little details may lead to serious consequences. As the seventeenth-century English poet George Herbert wrote:

> For want of a nail, a shoe was lost;
> For want of a shoe, a horse was lost;
> For want of a horse, a rider was lost;
> For want of a rider, a message was lost;
> For want of a message, a battle was lost;
> For want of a battle, a kingdom was lost;
> All for want of a nail.

The Old Testament book, Song of Solomon, speaks of "the little foxes that ruin the vineyards" (Song 2:15b). Many marriages get into trouble because spouses ignore the little details, the day-by-day thoughtfulness that strengthens their relationship as well as the "little foxes" of neglect, discontent, and unresolved issues that eat away at the "vineyard" of their happiness. Married couples need to give due attention to both in order to help ensure the long-term success, health, and vitality of their marriage.

Rebuke but Don't Criticize

One of the most dangerous of the "little foxes" to be let to run loose in the marital "vineyard" is criticism. Nothing shuts down communication and disrupts the harmony of a relationship faster than harsh, sniping, negative comments. No one profits from criticism—neither the critic nor the person being criticized, or anyone else who may be within earshot. Constant criticism destroys a person's spirit. It breeds hurt, resentment, defensiveness, and even hatred. Criticism discourages openness and honesty, without which no relationship can remain healthy. By its very nature criticism is destructive because it focuses on finding fault with the intention of hurting rather than of finding a solution. People who are critical all the time usually have unmet needs or unresolved issues in their own lives, and these problems reveal themselves in the form of a critical spirit.

 Nothing shuts down communication and disrupts the harmony of a relationship faster than harsh, sniping, negative comments.

Every relationship at times faces interpersonal conflicts that must be dealt with for the good of everyone involved. Part of effective communication is establishing an environment in which problems can be resolved in a healthy manner. Hurtful criticism is never the answer. Rather, in such situations a rebuke may be in order.

Criticism and rebuke are not the same thing. A rebuke differs from criticism in at least two important ways: the spirit from which it comes and the purpose for which it is given. Criticism arises from a wounded and self-centered spirit that seeks to wound in return. It is not interested in either the welfare of the person being criticized or in finding a constructive solution to the problem. A rebuke, on the other hand, comes from a loving and compassionate spirit that not only recognizes a problem but also seeks a fair and equitable solution with a heartfelt desire for the good of the other person. In short, a rebuke is motivated by love, whereas criticism is not. A rebuke focuses on the solution while criticism harps on the problem. A rebuke seeks to correct while criticism only complains.

Watch out for the "little fox" of criticism that can nibble away at your relationship. Develop the discipline of thinking before speaking. Whenever a problem arises or a conflict flares up and you feel the urge to criticize, ask yourself if it is a legitimate problem for which rebuke and correction are in order, or only a personal gripe. Check your motivation: Are you acting out of love or out of anger?

Criticism profits nothing, but rebuke and correction do. There are two sides to this coin, however. Being willing and able to give correction is one side; being willing to receive correction is the other. Openness to correction is one of the most important elements of growth. People who are unwilling to receive correction will never grow. They will always be immature.

 Openness to correction is one of the most important elements of growth.

Don't Get Too Familiar

Another "little fox" to watch out for is the "fox" of familiarity. One of the greatest dangers to a marriage is for the husband

and wife to become too familiar with each other. This is not the same as knowing each other. Spouses should know each other better and more intimately than they know anyone else in the world. A husband and wife should be each other's best friend. By familiarity I mean a comfortable complacency that causes a husband and wife to start taking each other for granted.

Familiarity reveals itself in at least three ways. First, it breeds ignorance. Couples feel so familiar with each other that they begin to ignore each other in lots of little ways that they may not even be aware of. Second, familiarity breeds assumptions. A husband and wife begin to assume that each knows what the other is thinking. The husband assumes not only that his wife knows what he is thinking but also that he knows what she is thinking. The wife makes the same assumptions. Third, familiarity breeds presumption. A wife will make a presumption regarding what her husband will say or do without even asking him first. A husband will make the same mistake with regard to his wife. If these three continue long enough the end result will be that as expressed in the old proverb, "Familiarity breeds contempt."

Here's a practical example of how this happens. Before marriage, when a couple is courting, they constantly tell each other how they feel. They don't assume anything. They pay attention to every little detail, every nuance of voice, every gesture and facial expression. They never presume to second-guess each other. They talk sweet things to each other on the phone for three hours and, meeting in person an hour later, spend two more hours saying more of the same. They compliment each other, give each other gifts, and spend every available moment together.

This constant attention to each other is good and necessary to building a strong relationship because it produces in each person a deep sense of security. They feel secure in each other's love and affection so that even when they are apart they still bask in the warmth of the knowledge that someone loves and cares about them. The more often we are told that we are loved, the more secure we feel.

For some reason, things begin to change after a couple gets married. It usually does not happen right away. Gradually the husband and wife start to assume things about each other. The husband stops saying to his wife, "I love you," as often as he once did. He assumes, "She knows I love her. I don't need to tell her all the time." This may not even be a conscious thought. They stop going out to dinner or on other dates. They stop giving "just because I love you" gifts or cards or flowers to each other. They have become comfortable together, and this comfort breeds a familiarity that can cause them to slowly drift apart without even realizing it.

When a married couple becomes too familiar with each other, a lot of the adventurous spontaneity goes out of their marriage. Marriage should be stable and strong so that both partners feel secure, but within that environment there should always be room for adventure. One excellent way to keep a marriage alive and vital and exciting is for the husband and wife both to be spontaneous at times—to do something unexpected. It may be something big, like a weekend away just the two of them, or something small and simple, like a candlelight dinner or a bouquet of flowers "just because." The key is to avoid familiarity and predictability by never taking each other for granted. Among other things, this means developing the practice of regularly expressing appreciation for each other.

 When a married couple becomes too familiar with each other, a lot of the adventurous spontaneity goes out of their marriage.

Express Honest Appreciation

Learning to appreciate people is one of the most effective ways to create an environment for open communication, as well as one of the most important nutrients for building healthy relationships. Appreciation involves being aware of what others do for us, letting them know that we recognize it, and thanking them for it. It also means praising someone for his or her accomplishments with sincere happiness at his or her success. It is very easy to be critical or to become jealous over another's achievements or attention. Most of us have to work at being appreciative because it goes against our selfish human nature.

One important thing that expressing honest appreciation does for us is to keep us mindful of our dependence upon each other. None of us ever achieves success or happiness by ourselves. There are people all along our path of life who help us on our way, and often it is easy to ignore or overlook their contribution. Nowhere is this truer than in marriage. Humanly speaking, a husband's greatest asset for success and happiness is his wife, and a wife's, her husband. They should be each other's greatest supporter, promoter, and encourager. No matter what happens in other circles, a couple's home should always be a place where they can find consistent love, appreciation, and affirmation.

Spouses who maintain a regular practice of expressing their love and appreciation to each other, even during good times when it is easy to take these things for granted, will discover that this deep sense of security will sustain them through bad times as well. Knowing that we are loved and appreciated by *someone* helps put in perspective the rest of life with all of its ups and downs. I can remember days when everything seemed to go wrong—nothing was working right at the office; some people canceled appointments while others did not follow through with what they said they would do. The car ran out of gas, then had a flat tire in the middle of a pouring rain. In times like those the only thing that kept me going was the secure knowledge that I had a wonderful woman at home—my wife—who loved me and cared about me.

Expressing honest appreciation regularly is so important to marital health that we cannot afford to leave it strictly to our emotions. Sometimes we don't feel like being appreciative. We may be tired or sick or angry or preoccupied. We must develop the habit of doing it anyway, based not on emotions but on knowledge. Emotions might say, "I don't feel like it," or "Don't bother me right now," whereas knowledge would say, "He *needs* to be affirmed right now," or "She *needs* me to reassure her that everything is all right."

Men generally have more of a problem with this than women do. For some reason, a lot of men have the idea that expressing their feelings openly and frequently to their wives is somehow unmasculine and a sign of weakness. On the contrary, there is nothing unmanly about a husband saying often to his wife, "Honey, I love you." A man who does this is displaying strength, not weakness. It takes more strength for a man to make himself vulnerable and expose his tender side than it does to put up a false "macho" façade that says, "I'm tough; I don't need to say that kind of stuff."

That's not acting tough; that's acting stupid because not even God takes that stance with us, and He is a lot bigger and a lot smarter than we are. Every day in many ways God tells us and shows us that He loves us. He does not leave it to chance. He knows we need to be reassured of it all the time. Those who are believers and followers of Christ know by experience that the Holy Spirit gives daily affirmation of God's love.

Husbands and wives need to get into the habit of expressing their love and appreciation for each other on a *daily* basis. Living under the same roof and sharing the same bed are no proof of love. Just ask any of the thousands of affection-starved men and women who endure unhappy marriages day after day.

Love is fed by love, not time. We need to get so used to expressing love and appreciation for each other that we feel uncomfortable whenever we *don't* do it. Honest love and appreciation are the lifeblood of a happy marriage. Don't take them for granted.

 Husbands and wives need to get into the habit of expressing their love and appreciation for each other on a daily basis.

Don't Ever Assume Love

Love needs to be expressed regularly and often; it should never be assumed. Husband, never assume that your wife knows that you love her; *tell her*! Even if you told her yesterday, tell her again, today. She needs to hear it every day. Wife, don't assume that your husband knows that you love him; *tell him*! Even though he may never come right out and say it, he needs that reassurance from you. No matter how tough and strong he may appear on the outside, he still needs you to tell him that you love him. We humans have a built-in need to be affirmed in this on a daily basis. Where love is concerned, there is no room for assumption.

In this, as in everything else, Jesus provides us with a wonderful example. Ephesians 5:21-33 teaches that husbands and wives are to relate to each other the way Christ and the Church—His Bride—relate to each other. Verse 25 says that "Christ loved the church and gave Himself up for her." This is a reference to His death on the cross. In John 15:13 Jesus told His followers, "Greater love has no one than this, that he lay down his life for his friends." Jesus' death on the cross for us was the greatest expression of love in history. Even so, Jesus never assumed that the example of His death alone would be enough to keep us assured of His love for all time. He knew that we needed daily reassurance. This is one reason why after

His resurrection He sent the Holy Spirit to dwell in all who believed in Him.

As recorded in the Gospel of John, Jesus refers to the Holy Spirit as a "Counselor" or "Comforter" (see Jn. 14:16,26; 15:26; 16:7 KJV). The Greek word is *parakletos*, which literally means "one who is called alongside." One important role of the "Comforter" is to "comfort" or reassure us on a daily basis of Christ's love for us. This is what Paul was referring to when he wrote, "God has poured out His love into our hearts by the Holy Spirit, whom He has given us" (Rom. 5:5b). For those who believe and follow Christ, the Holy Spirit resides permanently in their hearts and lives as a continual reminder of the love of God. Jesus gives us constant reassurance of His love; He never assumes that we know it.

Neither should we ever assume that our spouses know that we love them. Love may indeed "spring eternal," but our expression of it needs to be refreshed every day. We need to say it to our loved ones, and we need to hear them say it to us. Once, or even once in a while, is not enough. Here is an example.

Suppose a husband bought his wife a nice new car as an expression of his love for her. She is so excited and overjoyed with it, and he is pleased to be able to provide it. A few days later she asks, "Honey, do you love me?" A little surprised at her question, he answers, "I bought you that car, didn't I?" Several months later she asks again, "Honey, do you love me?" Again he replies, "I bought you that car, didn't I?" A year goes by, then another, and another, and it is always the same thing. Finally, 15 years later, the wife asks, "Honey, do you love me?" "I bought you that car, didn't I?"

Love may indeed "spring eternal," but our expression of it needs to be refreshed every day.

Doesn't that sound ridiculous? Yet, this is not too far from the truth with many marriages. Some people go weeks, months, and even years with no tangible expression of love from their spouses, either verbal or otherwise. In our minds, yesterday's act of love does not necessarily carry over to today. We all need daily reassurance.

Although verbal expression accounts for only 7 percent of what we communicate when we interact with one another, it is still one of the most important elements for feeding and nurturing love, especially for women. Men thrive on what they see, women thrive on what they hear, and both thrive on what they feel. Words reinforce actions, and women need to *hear* words of love, affection, and appreciation from their husbands.

Most men don't spend enough time simply *talking* to their wives. Over the years I have counseled hundreds of couples who were on the verge of divorce over this very issue. I could not begin to count the number of times I have had a conversation with the husband that runs something like this:

"Do you talk to your wife?"

"Well, she knows I love her. I don't have to talk to her and tell her that. After all, I buy her rings and other nice things."

"I didn't ask you what you *bought* her. Do you *talk* to her?"

"She knows I love her."

"You're making an assumption."

"Look, I buy food for her and the kids, and…"

"I didn't ask you that. Do you *talk* to her?"

"Well, I bought her flowers on Mother's Day. I'm sure she knows I love her because of that."

"You're assuming again, and you're also presuming that your gifts equal your love, but that's not true."

Giving *things* is no proof of our love. We must give *ourselves* first. That's exactly what Jesus did; He gave Himself for us. Then we must verbalize our love. We must make our words match our actions. If we do not communicate our love verbally, we can end up confusing the difference between the thing and the person. We must learn to appreciate each other, communicate with each other, and talk to each other. Talking is the strongest way to attach meaning to our actions. We must be careful never to assume *anything* in our relationships, especially love.

Pay "Little Attentions"

Any happily married couple will be quick to agree that their happiness is due in large part to simple daily thoughtfulness— little attentions that they pay to each other on an ongoing basis. These can take many forms. Compliments are always in order, whether referring to a well-cooked meal, a promotion at work, a fetching new hairstyle, a completed painting or poem, or whatever it might be. Honest gratitude sincerely expressed is always a winner. What reasonable person could reject a heartfelt "thank you"? Unfortunately, because it is so easy for married couples to slip into the rut of taking each other for granted, compliments and thank-yous are often in short supply and overlooked in many households.

Usually, common sense is our best guide where daily thoughtfulness is concerned, coupled with consistent application of the "Golden Rule": "Do to others as you would have them do to you" (Lk. 6:31). In other words, treat others the way you would like to be treated. Show others the same thoughtfulness and consideration that you would want them to show you.

Don't wait for someone else to show consideration for you. Be proactive in this; set the example yourself. If you have agreed to pick your wife up at a certain time and find yourself running late, stop somewhere and give her a call, even if your tardiness is unavoidable and for a good reason. Don't assume that she knows that you have been unavoidably delayed. Be true to your word. If circumstances force a change in your plans, let her know. She deserves that courtesy. Besides, that little extra effort of consideration and communication will prevent misunderstanding and an unpleasant argument later.

Think about the kinds of things that make you happy or make you feel loved and secure, and do those same things for your spouse. Iron his shirts just the way he likes. Send her flowers "just because." Write secret love notes and hide them in his sock drawer or in his shirt or pants pocket, or in her jewelry box, or in other unexpected places around the house that your spouse will be sure to look every now and then. Sure, it takes time to write these notes, but the rewards reaped in marital harmony and happiness will be well worth the time invested.

Let your imagination go. Be creative. Find ways to surprise and delight your spouse with "random acts of thoughtfulness." Paying little attentions will help keep romance and the spirit of courtship alive in your relationship, even after many years of marriage.

 Find ways to surprise and delight your spouse with "random acts of thoughtfulness."

Always Show Courtesy

Above all, always be courteous. Everyone deserves to be shown basic human kindness and dignity because we are all created in the image of God. Spouses should extend more courtesy to each other than they do to anyone else, yet courtesy often is one of the first things to fall into neglect in a marriage once a couple has become "familiar" with each other.

Courtesy works both ways. Wives should be just as courteous toward their husbands as they desire and expect their husbands to be toward them. Husbands, open the car door for her. Pull out the chair for her at the restaurant. Always treat her as if you were still courting her. After all, why would the things that won her heart in the first place not still be appropriate to keep her heart? In every situation, both public and private, show her the utmost respect. She deserves nothing less, and you will lift her in esteem before the world, making it clear to everyone that she is more important to you than anyone else.

Wives, don't be too proud or too "liberated" to allow your husband to extend such simple courtesies to you. Otherwise you will destroy his ability and opportunity to bless you. God created the male to find his fulfillment in blessing and giving of himself to the female. Don't deny him the chance to fulfill himself by fulfilling you.

Always be courteous toward your husband, respecting him in speech and in action, especially in public. This is not a demeaning deference as a servant to a master, but the esteem of one equal partner toward the other. Men especially need to be esteemed in the eyes of their colleagues and peers, and no one can do that better than their wives. Take advantage of every opportunity to support him and lift him up and encourage him.

Whenever a husband and wife are together in public, there should never be any doubt in anyone's mind that the two of them share a relationship characterized by mutual love, esteem, and respect. These qualities are nurtured and strengthened by the little things—not criticizing, showing honest appreciation, clearly expressing love, paying little attentions, and extending common courtesies—that they build into their marriage from the beginning.

 Don't forget the little things. They are the building blocks for the big things.

Don't forget the little things. They are the building blocks for the big things—things like effective communication; growth of genuine love; and firm establishment of harmony, happiness, and lifelong success in marriage.

PRINCIPLES

1. Ultimate success in marriage depends largely on giving attention to the "little things"—those simple, ongoing, daily courtesies and considerations that enhance communication and add sweetness to a relationship.

2. By its very nature criticism is destructive because it focuses on finding fault with the intention of hurting rather than of finding a solution.

3. A rebuke comes from a loving and compassionate spirit that not only recognizes a problem but also seeks a fair and equitable solution with a heartfelt desire for the good of the other person.

4. One of the greatest dangers to a marriage is for the husband and wife to become too familiar with each other—to take each other for granted.

5. One excellent way to keep a marriage alive and vital and exciting is for the husband and wife both to be spontaneous at times—to do something unexpected.

6. Honest love and appreciation are the lifeblood of a happy marriage.

7. Love needs to be expressed regularly and often; it should never be assumed.

8. Paying little attentions will help keep romance and the spirit of courtship alive in the relationship, even after many years of marriage.

9. Above all, always be courteous.

CHAPTER FIVE

Kingdom Management Principles for Couples

*I*f there is any single area of married life that causes more problems for couples than any other, it would have to be resource management. Although it certainly includes financial matters, resource management goes far beyond simply the question of how a couple handles their money. Resource management impinges on every facet of a couple's life together: employment and job choices; spending, saving, and investing money; career, professional, and educational goals; future dreams; and even family planning.

Another word for resource management is *stewardship*. A steward is one who manages the assets and affairs of another person. Although not the owner of those assets, a steward generally has wide latitude and authority in managing them on behalf of the owner. Continued stewardship is contingent upon the steward's faithfulness and effectiveness in representing the owner's interests. Successful stewards bring growth and increase of the assets under their charge, leading frequently to their being entrusted with even more assets and greater responsibility.

This principle is clearly taught throughout the pages of the Scriptures. One of the best biblical pictures of stewardship is seen in the life of Joseph. Genesis chapters 37–50 tell how Joseph was sold into slavery by his treacherous brothers, yet rose to become the most powerful government official in Egypt, second only to the pharaoh. As a slave of the captain of Pharaoh's bodyguard, Joseph proved himself a faithful and effective administrator of his master's estate, which prospered greatly under his stewardship.

Even after he was falsely accused of trying to rape his master's wife and was thrown into prison, Joseph continued to be faithful. The chief jailer recognized Joseph's gifts and integrity and placed him in charge of all the other prisoners. Once again, Joseph ably managed all that was placed under his care.

Eventually, the day came when Joseph's gifts drew the attention of the pharaoh himself. Impressed with the young man's wisdom, integrity, and obvious administrative abilities, the pharaoh elevated Joseph from slave to prime minister of all Egypt. Joseph's skillful management in this position made the most of seven years of bumper-crop prosperity and carried the nation successfully through the seven years of severe famine that followed. During this time he was also instrumental in saving the members of his own family from starvation— including the brothers who had treated him so cruelly so many years before.

Joseph prospered as a steward because he was faithful to his God and because he was faithful in his management of the resources entrusted to him. Recognizing that God was the true owner of all things, Joseph took great care to discharge his responsibilities in an honorable manner.

What does all this have to do with success and longevity in marriage? Simply this: Good stewardship is a solid biblical principle for growth, prosperity, and happiness. Too many married couples struggle financially and in other areas because they have an inadequate understanding of the truth that, as Creator, God is the owner of all things and that they are merely stewards and responsible to Him for how they manage the resources He places in their charge.

Designed for Stewardship

Stewardship is woven into the very fabric of God's original design for human life and experience. When God created mankind—male and female—He gave them dominion "over the fish of the sea and the birds of the air, over the livestock, over all the earth, and over all the creatures that move along the ground" (Gen. 1:26b). The essence of dominion is rulership. God created men and women to rule over the created order as equal partners under His supreme sovereignty. He charged mankind with the responsibility of being stewards of the earth and all its resources. Even though in the garden context of creation this equal partnership is seen through the framework of marriage, the kingdom management principles revealed there apply in every setting and circumstance and to all persons, whether male or female, married or single.

 Stewardship is woven into the very fabric of God's original design for human life and experience.

To exercise dominion over the earth means to govern, control, or rule over it; it is to gain mastery over it. Mastery over the earth does not mean untrammeled exploitation and waste of resources but careful and wise management of them. Properly administered, dominion always involves management. Our dominion as humans extends throughout the earth and covers all the lower creatures, but it stops short of ruling over each other. Certainly, human society maintains governments, elected officials, and chains of command and authority to help sustain order, but these are legitimate only as far as they exercise their authority with the choice and consent of the people. God did not create any of us for the purpose of dominating anyone else, but He *did* create *all* of us for the purpose of dominating and managing the earth and its resources. We have dominion over *things*, not people.

There are schools of management today that teach us how to manage other people, but many of them actually focus on manipulating people, on "stroking" them and deceiving them into doing what we want them to do, regardless of their desires. This approach is motivated by a desire to control and even oppress other people, which is contrary to the will of God.

As humans, our original responsibility was administration; God built that capacity into us. He did not reserve dominion for a few specially favored and elite people, but opened it up for the entire human race. By God's express design, the seeds of greatness, the potential for leadership, and the basic capability for management and administration exist in each of us.

> *So God created man in His own image, in the image of God He created him; male and female He created them. God blessed them and said to them, "Be fruitful and increase in number; fill the earth and subdue it. Rule over the fish of the sea and the birds of the air and over every living creature that moves on the ground"* (Genesis 1:27-28).

God never demands anything that He does not provide for. Whatever God commands us to do, He equips us to do. Before He said, "Be fruitful and increase in number; fill the earth and subdue it," He implanted the ability to do those things into the very fiber of our being.

The Lord of creation designed us for stewardship. Our original purpose was to rule over and manage the domain called Earth. Whenever we do not do what God created us to do, we suffer. Failure to fulfill our purpose often leads to poverty of spirit and mind, as well as of body. Apart from our divine design we fail to prosper. We may become frustrated, or even severely depressed.

Failure to fulfill our purpose often leads to poverty of spirit and mind, as well as of body.

On the other hand, those who discover their God-given purpose and seek to live it out experience health, happiness, fulfillment, and satisfaction in every area of life, even in spite of hardships or challenges that come along the way. This is just as true for married couples as it is for individuals. Many marriages struggle and fail to prosper as they should because the couples have never understood their purpose as stewards of God's resources or learned to apply His Kingdom management principles.

God Is Looking for Managers

From the very beginning, the God of creation established management as a fundamental principle governing life on earth and the relationship of human beings to the rest of the created order. Growth and development are dependent upon effective management—upon stewardship. Without management there is no growth. This relationship is revealed in the second chapter of Genesis.

> *When the Lord God made the earth and the heavens—and no shrub of the field had yet appeared on the earth and no plant of the field had yet sprung up, for the Lord God had not sent rain on the earth and there was no man to work the ground, but streams came up from the earth and watered the whole surface of the ground—the Lord God formed the man from the dust of the ground and breathed into his nostrils the breath of life, and the man became a living being* (Genesis 2:4b-7).

Notice the progression indicated in these verses. Although God had already created the earth, no plants of the field had yet appeared for two reasons: no rain had fallen on the earth and "there was no man to work the ground." God withheld development until a manager was in place. Life could flourish fully only when a steward appeared to take care of it.

Poor management retards growth. God holds back progress until He has management. He allows no increase until He has someone who can manage the increase; no expansion until He has someone who is accountable for that expansion.

 Poor management retards growth. God holds back progress until He has management.

God created man not because He needed a "religious" creature—someone to sing or dance or pray to Him—but because He needed someone to manage the planet. What we do during our worship services does not excite or interest God as much as what we do *afterwards*. He wants to see how well we manage our affairs: how we spend our time, what we do with our money, how wisely or how foolishly we use the resources at our disposal. He is looking for increase because good management always produces increase.

Wise management attracts God. If we are faithful with a little, God will entrust us with more. This too is a biblical principle. One day Jesus told a story about a wealthy man who went away on a long trip, leaving a different sum of money with each of three servants, according to their abilities (see Mt. 25:14-30). The first two servants went out immediately and, through careful management and wise investing, doubled their money. The third servant, however, did nothing except hide his money until his master returned. Upon his return, the master praised the first two servants for their faithfulness and increase, but he condemned the third servant for his poor stewardship. Ordering that the third servant's money be taken from him and given to the first servant, the master said, "For everyone who has will be given more, and he will have an abundance. Whoever does not have, even what he has will be taken from him" (Mt. 25:29).

 Wise management attracts God. If we are faithful with a little, God will entrust us with more.

If we hope to become effective and successful in life, ministry, and especially marriage, we have to learn to be good managers. Stewardship means being accountable to God for every resource under our care. Effective managers do more than simply keep things running; they add value to everything they have responsibility over. Under a good manager, resources will appreciate in value. The third servant in Jesus' story was punished not because he lost his master's money (he didn't; he still had it) but because he did nothing with it. He was judged because he added no value—brought no increase—to the resources entrusted to him.

All married couples should examine themselves periodically and ask, "What have we done with the resources God has given us? How are we handling His blessings? Are we spending our money wisely? Have we progressed over the past year? Are we moving in the direction God wants us to go? Are we obeying His will? Is He pleased with our management? What does He want us to do next?" These are important questions for growing in stewardship.

Dominion Is a Result of Stewardship

One key to growth in this area is for couples to understand that effective stewardship is not static but a developing process. This is how it was with the first human couple in the Garden of Eden. Genesis 1:28 reveals the progression: "God blessed them and said to them, 'Be fruitful and increase in number; fill the earth and subdue it. Rule over the fish of the sea and the birds of the air and over every living creature that moves on the ground.'" God's purpose for mankind was for them to rule over the created order, but to fulfill that purpose they first had to be fruitful, increase, fill, and subdue. Only then would humanity attain full dominion. Essentially, dominion is not a goal as much as it is the *result* of the fourfold process of fruitfulness, increase, filling, and subduing.

The first thing God did was to *bless* mankind—the male and female He had created. To bless means to release ability. By blessing them God released their ability to become what He had created them to be. He released them to be stewards of the earth and its resources. Then He instructed them on *how* to exercise dominion.

 Dominion is not a goal as much as it is the result of the fourfold process of fruitfulness, increase, filling, and subduing.

Be fruitful. God's command in Genesis 1:28 is most often understood as referring to procreation, but filling the earth with people is only part of the meaning. The Hebrew word for *fruitful* means more than just sexual reproduction; it refers to being fruitful in either a literal or a figurative sense. Fruitfulness can be qualitative in nature as well as quantitative. Mankind has never had a problem being procreative—a current global population of over 6 billion is proof of that—but we do have a problem with being fruitful in the other ways God desires.

Essentially, being fruitful means releasing our potential. Fruit is an end product. An apple tree may provide cool shade and be beautiful to look at, but until it produces apples it has not fulfilled its ultimate purpose. Apples contain the seeds of future apple trees and, therefore, future apples. However, apples also have something else to offer: a sweet and nourishing food to satisfy human physical hunger. In this sense, fruit has a greater purpose than simply reproducing; fruit exists to bless the world.

Every person is born with a seed of greatness. God never tells us to go find seed; it is already within us. Inside each of us is the seed potential for a full forest—a bumper crop of fruit with which to bless the world. We each were endowed at birth with a unique gift, something we were born to do or become that no one else can achieve the way we can. God's purpose is that we bear abundant fruit and release the blessings of our gift and potential to the world.

 Every person is born with a seed of greatness.

The tragic truth is that cemeteries are filled with unreleased orchards—people who died with their gift still locked inside of them in seed form. This is where the human race so often fails to fulfill God's command to "be fruitful." The world is forever poorer because of the countless millions who died without releasing their blessings.

Don't ever make the mistake of telling God that you have nothing to offer. That simply is not true. God does not create any junk. Every one of us is pregnant with seed, and God wants us to let our seed sprout, grow, and produce abundant fruit. He wants us to develop our seed to an edible phase, where the world can partake and be nourished and blessed.

What is your seed? Can you cook really well? Can you paint? Can you write? Do you have good business sense? Consider your combined gifts as a married couple. What financial and other physical or material resources has God entrusted to you? Do you have the gifts and abilities to start your own business? Are you equipped to work together in a unique or much-needed ministry? What professional and personal resources can you bring to bear to fulfill the purpose God placed in you when you were born? You have something the world needs. Be fruitful. Let the Spirit of God bring out of you what your Creator put in you.

Increase. Being fruitful is a good and necessary start, but it should grow into the next phase, *increase*. Once again, even though the idea here is to multiply or reproduce, sexual procreation is only part of the meaning. The Hebrew word for *increase* also can mean "abundance," "to be in authority," "to enlarge," and "to excel." It carries the sense of refining your gift until it is completely unique. It is impossible to reproduce what you have not refined.

In this context, then, to increase means not only to multiply or reproduce as in having children, but also to improve and excel, mastering your gift and becoming the very best you can possibly be at what you do. It also means learning how to manage the resources God has given you and developing a strategy for managing the increase that will come through refinement. By refining your gift, you make room for it in the world. The more refined your gift, the more in demand you will be. Proverbs 18:16 (KJV) says, "A man's gift maketh room for him, and bringeth him before great men."

 By refining your gift, you make room for it in the world.

What is your fruit—your gift? What are you known for? What do you have that is reproducible? What quality or ability do you have that causes people to seek you out? What brings you joy? What are you passionate about? What do you have to offer the world, even just your little part of it?

Fruit must be reproducible or else it is not genuine fruit. "Be fruitful" means to produce fruit; "increase" means to reproduce it.

Fill. The third phase of dominion is to "fill" or "replenish" the earth. Bearing fruit, refining our gift, and mastering the use of our resources create demand and lead naturally to wider "distribution." To "fill the earth" means to expand our gift, our influence, our resources, just as a growing business would by continually improving its product, opening new outlets, and hiring more employees.

Another way to look at it is to think once again of an apple tree. A single apple seed grows into an apple tree, which then produces apples, each of which contains seeds for producing more trees. Planting those seeds soon turns a single apple tree into a whole orchard.

This expansion to "fill the earth" is a joint effort between the Lord and us. Our part is to be faithful with the resources He has given. He is the one who brings the expansion. The more faithful we are with our stewardship, the more resources God will entrust to us. That is a biblical principle.

Subdue. Fruitfulness, increase, and filling lead naturally to the end result of subduing. To *subdue* means "to dominate or control," not in the negative sense of oppression, but in the positive sense of administration. Using business terminology, to subdue means to dominate the market. As we learn to manage our resources, God expands those resources and enlarges our influence. He increases our "market share," so to speak.

There is no limit to what the Lord can do in and with and through any individual or any married couple who surrender themselves and their resources completely to His will and His way. He wants to cover the world with His "orchards" of human fruitfulness. Habakkuk 2:14 says, "For the earth will be filled with the knowledge of the glory of the Lord, as the waters cover the sea," and the Lord is fulfilling that promise one person at a time and one couple at a time.

> *There is no limit to what the Lord can do in and with and through any individual or any married couple who surrender themselves and their resources completely to His will and His way.*

Two Important Financial Principles

Basic stewardship of resources for married couples who are believers centers around understanding and practicing two fundamental financial principles: tithing and budgeting. Herein lie the seeds of dominion—the secrets of fruitfulness, increase, and filling. Tithing recognizes God as the source of our resources while budgeting recognizes our responsibility to God to manage those resources wisely.

Rather than a rigid, legalistic designation of 10 percent of "our" income to God performed out of a sense of duty, tithing at its heart is a freely given offering of "firstfruits" in recognition that God is the Creator and true owner of *everything* that we have. It reminds us not to hold on to our possessions too tightly because we are merely stewards, not owners. It helps us keep our priorities in proper perspective, so that we do not make the mistake of allowing our possessions and pursuit of prosperity to supercede our relationship with the Lord as first place in our lives. Indeed, tithing reminds us that God is the source and giver of our prosperity: "But remember the Lord your God, for it is He who gives you the ability to produce wealth" (Deut. 8:18a).

Tithing is an expression of seed faith that operates on the principle of blessings and returns. It demonstrates our trust in God's ability and promise to meet our needs day by day. For married couples who desire God's blessings and prosperity on their home and to see His power at work in their lives and daily influence, a commitment to tithing is indispensable. God has made His promise clear and unambiguous: "'Bring the whole tithe into the storehouse, that there may be food in My house. Test Me in this,' says the Lord Almighty, 'and see if I will not throw open the floodgates of heaven and pour out so much blessing that you will not have room enough for it'" (Mal. 3:10). This principle is operable at every level, in individuals, couples, families, and churches.

Tithing is an expression of seed faith that operates on the principle of blessings and returns.

Although giving is important, the attitude of the giver is more important. The amount we give is not as important to God as the spirit in which we give it. Jesus taught this lesson to His followers one day as they watched different people place their offerings in the temple treasury (see Mk. 12:41-44). Many who were wealthy gave large amounts of money while a poor widow dropped in only two coins, worth about a penny. Jesus commended the widow for her attitude of trust in God: "I tell you the truth, this poor widow has put more into the treasury than all the others. They all gave out of their wealth; but she, out of her poverty, put in everything—all she had to live on" (Mk. 12:43b-44).

The amount we give is not as important to God as the spirit in which we give it.

God desires that we give freely from a joyful heart rather than out of a sense of obligation, acknowledging Him as the source of our blessings. Paul, the great first-century missionary and New Testament writer, had this to say to the believers in the city of Corinth: "Each man should give what he has decided in his heart to give, not reluctantly or under compulsion, for God loves a cheerful giver" (2 Cor. 9:7).

Unfortunately, no matter how hard they try, many couples fail to achieve even the most basic level of prosperity or financial stability. More often than not, the primary reason for this is that they have never understood or settled within themselves the basic issue of tithing and the principle of blessings and returns.

God's program of prosperity does not operate on the world's principles. As long as we act as if we own our resources, we will tend to be very possessive of them and unwilling to release them for God's use. This will shut us off from His greater blessings, both the blessing of being used for His purpose and the blessing of being entrusted with greater resources. If as stewards we hold lightly to them, however, we can release them for the Lord's use as He leads and, by proving ourselves faithful with a little, He will entrust us with much.

Tithing should be one major facet of a couple's overall financial plan. Every household should operate on a budget, or financial plan. Budgeting is a basic principle of resource management. A household budget should be no more complex than needed to manage the family's resources effectively. Depending on a couple's circumstances, a simple ledger to keep track of income and expenses may be all that is necessary. Generally, the more complex a couple's assets, the more detailed their plan for managing them will need to be.

 A household budget should be no more complex than needed to manage the family's resources effectively.

The complexity of the family budget also will depend upon the dreams and plans of the couple. Do you want to buy a house? If so, you will need to initiate a clear plan for saving money regularly, as well as being very careful with your credit and with managing debt. Do you plan to invest? These plans need to be set out specifically in your budget or financial plan and you need to agree together as to how you are going to pursue your goals.

Don't neglect to budget "fun" money. Leisure and recreation are important for overall physical, mental, and emotional health, and they should be provided for in the budget. These do not have to be expensive, and a couple should certainly keep these costs in line with their financial means. Whether or not both the husband and wife work outside the home, each should have a regular "allowance" of money to spend entirely on their own.

The type or complexity of your financial plan is not as important as the fact that you have a plan of some kind in place and operating. As long as your budget is adequate for your needs, it doesn't matter what form it takes. A working budget represents good management and an honest effort at wise stewardship. God honors both.

PRINCIPLES

֎

1. Good stewardship is a solid biblical principle for growth, prosperity, and happiness.

2. God charged mankind with the responsibility of being stewards of the Earth and all its resources.

3. We have dominion over *things*, not people.

4. By God's express design, the seeds of greatness, the potential for leadership, and the basic capability for management and administration exist in each of us.

5. Stewardship means being accountable to God for every resource under our care.

6. Being fruitful means releasing our potential.

7. To increase means not only to multiply or reproduce as in having children, but also to improve and excel, mastering our gift and becoming the very best we can possibly be at what we do.

8. To "fill the earth" means to expand our gift, our influence, our resources, just as a growing business would by continually improving its product, opening new outlets, and hiring more employees.

9. To subdue means to "dominate the market."

10. Tithing recognizes God as the source of our resources.

11. Budgeting recognizes our responsibility to God to manage those resources wisely.

CHAPTER SIX

Sexual Intimacy in Marriage

Although effective resource management may be the most practical challenge that the majority of married couples face, achieving fully satisfying sexual intimacy is probably the most personal. Many couples are confused about their sexuality, not so much with regard to their sexual identities as with understanding how to properly relate to each other sexually. Sexual dysfunction is a significant source of frustration, conflict, and unhappiness in many marriages. Often dissatisfaction with sex is one of the root causes of spouses entering into extramarital affairs. What they are not getting at home they look for elsewhere. Quite often, this sexual confusion stems from a basic lack of understanding of both the true nature and purpose of sex as well as the proper conditions for fulfilling sexual expression.

Unfortunately, conscientious couples looking for solid answers oftentimes have trouble finding them. Our modern sex-saturated society is certainly not much help. Although we live in a time when sexuality issues are discussed more openly and frankly than ever before, much of the popular discussion of sex is based on dreams, fantasy, and human ideas rather than on truth, reality, and the wisdom of the ages.

Everywhere we turn we are bombarded by sexual images and messages. Sex drives both the entertainment and the advertising industries. It fills the airwaves and the movie theaters. It is used to sell everything from shaving cream to automobiles. Even our everyday speech is peppered with sex talk. Some people seemingly cannot hold a conversation unless it is laced with sexual references. Yet, for all of our talking and thinking about sex, much of society remains largely ignorant of the subject because so much of our dialogue is based on error and misconceptions.

Another sad truth is that the modern Church typically has little to add to the discussion. This is especially tragic because believers, who know and follow the God who created sex and established its proper parameters, should be able to speak more intelligently and confidently about it than anyone else. Yet the community of believers is often silent in the public forum regarding sex, whether because of embarrassment, confusion, timidity, or a sense that the subject of sex is either too personal or not sufficiently "spiritual" for the Church to weigh in on publicly.

Sex is not a side issue with God. The Bible has much more to say on the subject of sex and sexual relations than most people are aware of. Sexuality is fundamental to God's design and plan for humanity. "So God created man in His own image, in the image of God He created him; *male and female* He created them" (Gen. 1:27 emphasis added). "Male and female" are gender distinctions that imply sexuality. Sex also lies at the very core of God's initial instructions to the first human couple to "be fruitful and increase in number; fill the earth and subdue it" (Gen. 1:28b). Although, as we saw in the previous chapter, this command deals essentially with dominion and the stewardship of resources, it certainly also includes sexual activity as a fundamental principle.

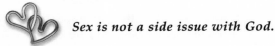 ***Sex is not a side issue with God.***

Because of its importance to human experience and because of the widespread confusion that exists on the subject today, it is crucial that we come to a biblical understanding of sexuality in order to counter the errors and misinformation that are so prevalent in our society. We need to understand what sex is *not*, what it *is*, and what its purpose is, as well as establish guidelines for acceptable sexual activity within the context of a biblical marriage.

Sex Is Not Love

In the eyes of the world, sex and love are synonymous. Even the most casual perusal of today's newspapers, magazines, books, movies, and television programs will make this clear. Much of the material in these media treats sex and love as if they are inseparable, as if there is no difference between them. The logical outflow of this view is the philosophy that says, "If you love me, you'll let me." After all, if sex and love are the same, how can you claim to love someone and yet decline to have sex with him or her?

Closely related to this is the view that sex is proof of love. How often do we encounter this scenario in books or on film: A man meets a woman and they hit it off well. The next thing we know, they are in bed together. This is our "tip off" that they are "in love." They must be in love; they're having sex, aren't they? It may be an adulterous relationship with one or both of them married to someone else, but that doesn't matter. All that matters is that they are in love. They go to bed, have their fling, get up the next morning, and everything is fine.

That's the picture the world paints. What these books and films rarely if ever reveal is the negative side to these kinds of encounters. In real life, sexual liaisons of this type produce in most people feelings of guilt, shame, and a sense of being dirty, not to mention a deep absence of fulfillment. It may be "fun" for a moment, but it leaves them feeling empty, and often they don't know why.

The idea of sex as love is one of the biggest lies with which the world has perverted God's original design for sexual expression, enjoyment, and fulfillment.

The idea of sex as love is one of the biggest lies with which the world has perverted God's original design for sexual expression, enjoyment, and fulfillment.

Sex Is Not Spiritual

Love—*true* love—is spiritual in nature. Sex is not. Sex is 100 percent physical and chemical. That is why we run into problems whenever we try to equate love with sex. Love is a spiritual union between two people—a joining of spirit to spirit. Sex is a physical coupling of two people—a joining of flesh to flesh. In its proper use, sex is a beautiful and fulfilling physical expression of the spiritual joining that is true love.

Love is a spiritual union between two people— a joining of spirit to spirit. Sex is a physical coupling of two people—a joining of flesh to flesh.

Understanding this distinction will help us guard against falling prey to a lot of the weird ideas floating around out there that try to convince us that sex is (or can be) some fantastic kind of "spiritual bonding" or getting in touch with the spiritual realities of life. It is nothing of the sort. Sex is an exhilarating physical experience, but in and of itself there is nothing spiritual about it. Sexual activity never bonds us spirit to spirit with another person. Nowhere does the Bible teach that a sexual experience will cause us to see God or be brought close to Him. Sex is a product of the human part of our makeup and has nothing to do with our spirit. Rather, our God-given sexual drive is an appetite that must be brought into subjection to and controlled by our spirit. Our spirit is to rule over our flesh.

Sex Is an Appetite

Sex is an appetite, one of many appetites that God built in to us when He created us. Whether we call them drives, cravings, hungers, passions, or whatever, they are still appetites. We have an appetite for food, an appetite for water, an appetite for sleep, an appetite for sex, an appetite for God—you name it. All of these are perfectly normal. God designed us for appetites.

The strength of any appetite is determined by the degree to which the capacity for that appetite has been activated. All appetites begin at a capacity level of zero. The ability for an appetite is always present, but its capacity will be zero until it is activated. A baby develops an appetite and capacity for food even before it is born as nourishment flows to it from the mother through the umbilical cord. That's why the very first thing a baby wants to do after it is born is to feed—its food appetite has been activated.

Although a newborn infant knows food hunger, its capacity is still low. A baby is hungry only for what its appetite has been activated for. Infants accustomed to liquid nourishment through the umbilical cord before birth and breast milk or formula and bland baby food afterwards have no craving for salt or other spices, or for sugar or any other kind of sweets. Those appetites are dormant until they are activated. Parents activate those appetites in their children by introducing them to seasoned foods and to cake, candy, and other sweet treats. Until then, a child has no appetite—and therefore no desire—for them.

The reason we get hungry is because chemicals in our stomach and digestive tract become active and signal our brain that we need food. Depending on how long it has been since we last ate, and other factors such as the kinds of foods we crave, our appetite capacity rises accordingly. Our sense of hunger will continue to grow until we satisfy it by eating. Once satisfied, our appetite falls off until it is reactivated when it is time to eat again. ·

An interesting thing happens, however, to an appetite that is left unsatisfied: Eventually it falls off anyway. People who enter into an extended fast quickly discover this. The earliest days of a fast are the hardest because our appetite for food has to be readjusted. After our body adapts, the fast is easier.

My point is this: Not only can we *satisfy* our appetites, we also can *control* them. *Every* appetite is like that. Our hungers and cravings are subject to our will. This is just as true for our sexual appetite as for any other. Paul made this clear in his first New Testament letter to the believers in the Asian city of Thessalonica when he wrote: "It is God's will that you should be sanctified: that you should avoid sexual immorality; that each of you should learn to control his own body in a way that is holy and honorable" (1 Thess. 4:3-4). What makes this passage even more interesting is that the Greek word *skeuos* ("body") also could be understood to mean "wife." In this sense, then, Paul would be saying that husbands should learn to "live with their own wives in a way that is holy and honorable." Either way, the emphasis is on controlling one's sexual appetite, reserving it for expression exclusively in the context of a marriage relationship.

 Our hungers and cravings are subject to our will. This is just as true for our sexual appetite as for any other.

God's Purposes for Sex

God created us as sexual beings, as male and female. Sexuality is built into our very core as humans. You could say that we are "hardwired" for sex. Appropriate and truly fulfilling sexual expression can occur only within the careful and specific limits that God has established. Outside those limits there is trouble—guilt, shame, fear, sorrow, disappointment, and heartache. Within those limits, however—the limits of one husband and one wife devoted exclusively to each other—there is great freedom, flexibility, and joy.

From the pages of the Bible we can glean three primary purposes for human sexual activity: procreation, recreation and release, and communication.

Sex Is for Procreation

As we have already seen, procreation lies at the very heart of God's original charge and command to mankind. "God blessed them and said to them, 'Be fruitful and increase in number; fill the earth and subdue it. Rule over the fish of the sea and the birds of the air and over every living creature that moves on the ground'" (Gen. 1:28). God created man to exercise dominion over the created order, and one way of accomplishing that goal was through procreation: to reproduce and populate the earth.

It was to this end that God created man in two genders, a male "man" and a female "man." The man and the woman were of the same spirit and the same essence—they were made of the same "stuff," as it were. First, God created the man, Adam. Then He made a woman—Eve—from part of Adam's side, and presented her to him. "The man said, 'This is now bone of my bones and flesh of my flesh; she shall be called "woman," for she was taken out of man.' For this reason a man will leave his father and mother and be united to his wife, and they will become one flesh" (Gen. 2:23-24). The phrase "one flesh" is a sexual reference relating to the physical union between a husband and wife.

The Bible contains many other references that indicate that human reproduction is a fundamental part of God's plan for mankind. In its proper place, sex is both honorable and a source of blessing from God.

> *If you pay attention to these laws and are careful to follow them, then the Lord your God will keep His covenant of love with you, as He swore to your forefathers. He will love you and bless you and increase your numbers.* **He will bless the fruit of your womb**, *the crops of your land—your grain, new wine and oil—the calves of your herds and the lambs of your flocks in the land that he swore to your forefathers to give you. You will be blessed more than any other people;* **none of your men or women will be childless**, *nor any of your livestock without young* (Deuteronomy 7:12-14 emphasis added).

Here God actually makes a commitment to His people that if they are faithful and obedient to Him, none of them will be barren or childless. God wants His people to procreate. He wants to populate the world with His children so that His glory will fill the earth.

> *Sons are a heritage from the Lord, children a reward from Him. Like arrows in the hands of a warrior are sons born in one's youth. Blessed is the man whose quiver is full of them. They will not be put to shame when they contend with their enemies in the gate* (Psalm 127:3-5).

Children are a heritage from God. The Hebrew word *ben* ("sons") has a wide variety of meanings and can refer to all children, not just males. Heritage means "property." God takes the conceiving, birthing, and raising of children very seriously because they are His heritage. That's why abortion and physical and sexual abuse of children are such serious sins— they are messing with God's heritage.

God takes the conceiving, birthing, and raising of children very seriously because they are His heritage.

There are many other passages that could be cited but these should be sufficient to demonstrate clearly—if there was any doubt—that one of the primary purposes of sex is for procreation.

Sex Is for Recreation and Release

If procreation is the practical, necessary side to sex, then recreation and release make up the "impractical" side. We have sex not only to reproduce the race but also for the sheer joy and pleasure it affords. Let's be frank: Sex is fun. God meant for us to enjoy sex; otherwise, why would He have designed it to be so pleasurable?

Some people, including many believers, are uncomfortable with such frankness where sex is concerned. They feel even more ill at ease at the thought of parts of the Bible—God's Word—being sexually explicit. Nevertheless, it is true that the Word of God contains some "racy" sections, particularly the book called the Song of Solomon (Song of Songs in the New International Version). This Old Testament book is so open and frank in its language that many believers have felt more comfortable allegorizing its content into a symbolic story about Christ's love for His Church. Perhaps it does indeed have that meaning as well, but at heart the Song of Solomon is a frank and explicit love song that celebrates the joy and bliss of married love.

 God meant for us to enjoy sex; otherwise, why would He have designed it to be so pleasurable?

One example will be sufficient to show how the Bible presents sex in marriage as a recreational pleasure apart from any reference to procreation.

How beautiful you are, my darling! Oh, how beautiful! Your eyes behind your veil are doves....Your lips are like a scarlet ribbon; your mouth is lovely....Your two breasts are like two fawns, like twin fawns of a gazelle that browse among the lilies....You have stolen my heart, my sister, my bride; you have stolen my heart with one glance of your eyes, with one jewel of your necklace. How delightful is your love, my sister, my bride! How much more pleasing is your love than wine, and the fragrance of your perfume than any spice! Your lips drop sweetness as the honeycomb, my bride; milk and honey are under your tongue. The fragrance of your garments is like that of Lebanon. You are a garden locked up, my sister, my bride; you are a spring enclosed, a sealed fountain. Your plants are an orchard of pomegranates with choice fruits, with henna and nard, nard and saffron, calamus and cinnamon, with every kind of incense tree, with myrrh and aloes and all the finest spices. You are a garden fountain, a well of flowing water streaming down from Lebanon. Awake, north wind, and come, south wind! Blow on my garden, that its fragrance may spread abroad. Let my lover come into his garden and taste its choice fruits (Song of Songs 4:1a,3a,5,9-16).

This is frank and intimate sex talk between two lovers, but the passage also makes it clear that they are husband and wife. Three times the man refers to his lover as "my sister, my bride." These verses describe the husband's relaxed, loving inventory of his wife's physical beauty. In verse 12, the phrases "a garden locked up," a spring enclosed," and "a sealed fountain" refer to the bride's virginity on her wedding night. In the eyes of her husband she is a garden of beauty, an orchard of "choice fruits," "incense," and "all the finest spices." Verse 16 is actually the bride's response to her husband's love talk, inviting him, her lover, to "come into his garden and taste its choice fruits."

If the explicit and intimate nature of this language shocks you, keep in mind that it does not shock God. God invented sex, and He wants us to experience its joys. *In the proper context of a loving marriage relationship*, there is nothing shameful, wrong, or immoral about sex. Sex is a pleasure meant to be enjoyed between a husband and wife for its own sake.

Sex Is for Communication

The third purpose for which God designed sex is communication. Sex is no substitute for open and honest conversation between a husband and wife, but in a loving environment that encourages communication, sexual consummation provides a degree of intimacy and communion that goes far beyond words. No one should be more intimate or more "connected" physically, mentally, or emotionally than a husband and wife. Their friendship should have no rival; no other earthly relationship should have higher priority. This is the essential meaning behind Genesis 2:24: "For this reason a man will leave his father and mother and be united to his wife, and they will become one flesh."

Under God's standard, sexual activity is restricted to marriage. The husband/wife relationship is a singular relationship, and sexual foreplay and intercourse provide a unique form of intimate communion and sharing that they should reserve exclusively for each other.

Be Responsive to Each Other's Sexual Needs

Sexual dysfunction and dissatisfaction in marriage often stem not so much from a husband's or wife's inability or unwillingness to "perform" sexually as to the couple's failure to be sensitive, aware, and responsive to each other's sexual needs. As with effective communication, remembering the little things is important where sex is concerned also.

We have to be willing to look beyond our own feelings and perspective to those of our spouse. Just because we may or may not desire sex at a particular moment does not necessarily mean that our spouse feels the same way. It would be unhealthy to our relationship to make that assumption. This is where mature, effective communication skills are very important. Sexual fulfillment and happiness in marriage depend on an open, loving, accepting, and affirming environment in which each spouse feels comfortable making his or her needs and desires known to the other.

Although there have been some significant changes in recent years, particularly in the west, it is still quite common in most societies for wives to feel very inhibited when it comes to initiating sex with their husbands. In some cultures it is unheard of for the wife to be so bold. In others, women are raised to believe that if they initiate sex, they are being "loose" or throwing themselves at the man. Whatever the reason, even if they crave sexual intimacy, wives often wait passively for their husbands to be the aggressor.

For his part, a husband may interpret his wife's passivity as disinterest and leave her alone because he does not want her to feel that he is forcing himself on her. As a result, both of them suffer through days, weeks, or even months of wandering in a sexual desert simply because they have failed to make their needs known to each other. If their uncommunicated needs go unmet long enough, they may seek sexual satisfaction outside their relationship.

It is very important that husbands and wives, and especially wives, learn to speak up regarding their sexual needs. Wives, as far as your husband is concerned, it is all right for you to be as "loose" as you want to be! If *you* are not "loose" with him, some other woman will be. Your husband has legitimate sexual needs and if you do not meet them, someone else will. Use your imagination! Be bold! Do something daring!

Don't be afraid to initiate a sexual encounter occasionally. Surprise your husband with your aggressiveness! Remember that as a man your husband is "hardwired" for visual stimulation and arousal. Give him something to be stimulated about!

By the same token, husbands, keep in mind that as a woman your wife is "hardwired" for tactile and aural stimulation and arousal. She craves your touch. Embrace her and hold her close. She needs you to *tell* her how beautiful she is, how sexy she is, and how much you love her, how much you desire her, and how much you need her! She loves to hear you whisper "sweet nothings" in her ear.

 It is very important that husbands and wives, and especially wives, learn to speak up regarding their sexual needs.

These may sound like small things, but they are the things that will keep the fire burning in a marriage. Husbands and wives have a responsibility to love each other at all times and to express that love sexually often enough to keep each other satisfied. Of course, how often is enough will depend on the couple. Sexual relations are a normal part of marriage that each spouse has the right to expect from the other as well as the responsibility to give to the other. Here is what the New Testament writer Paul had to say in this regard:

> *The husband should fulfill his marital duty to his wife, and likewise the wife to her husband. The wife's body does not belong to her alone but also to her husband. In the same way, the husband's body does not belong to him alone but also to his wife. Do not deprive each other except by mutual consent and for a time, so that you may devote yourselves to prayer. Then come together again so that Satan will not tempt you because of your lack of self-control* (1 Corinthians 7:3-5).

It is clear from the context of this passage that "marital duty" refers to sexual relations. Both the husband and the wife have the responsibility—the duty—to respond to each other sexually. Duty often takes precedence over feelings. Understanding this can help on those occasions when one partner is "in the mood" and the other is not. There are times when, regardless of our personal feelings, we will need to respond to our spouse out of love and responsibility.

Sexual relations are a normal part of marriage that each spouse has the right to expect from the other as well as the responsibility to give to the other.

Sometimes we forget that the little things in our sexual relationship are what make the whole marriage a complete fellowship and union. The little things are important to communicating our love to our spouse, and sometimes it has nothing to do with our feelings.

Does It Edify?

There is one final question we need to consider regarding sexual intimacy in marriage. Amidst the multiplicity of ideas and attitudes about sexual activity that exists in the world, many married couples today, especially believers, are confused to some extent as to what does and does not constitute appropriate sexual behavior for husbands and wives. What is moral, right, and proper, and what is not? This confusion is understandable since so many people come into marriage from a worldly background that promotes an "anything goes" approach to sex. In the eyes of secular society, nothing is taboo anymore. Masturbation, oral sex, anal sex, group sex, pornography, pedophilia, homosexuality, bestiality, sado-masochism— you name it—the world says, "If it's right for you, do it!"

The question we need to ask, however, is, "What does the Word of God say?" God invented sex. He designed it and established the guidelines, parameters, and limits under which it can be morally exercised. One fundamental principle of creation is the "fitness" principle. God created everything to "fit" in its proper place and in relation to everything else. This is just as true with human sexuality as with any other area of life. The male and female sexual organs were designed to "fit" and are ideally suited for their mutual function. Any activity that goes beyond the bounds of design function violates the "fitness" principle and amounts to perversion. Perversion simply means the abuse, misuse, or misrepresentation of the original purpose of a thing. This is why homosexuality, for example, is such a sin; it is a perversion of the original design function of human sexuality.

What constitutes inappropriate sexual behavior? Some people would say that for married couples, anything that they agree upon is okay. What goes on in a couple's bedroom is their private affair, but nothing is hidden from God. I think it is safe to say that there are certain types of behavior that are always inappropriate. Aside from those acts that violate the "fitness" principle, inappropriate sexual behavior would include anything that is deliberately physically painful, harmful, or unhealthy, as well as any sexual act that one partner forces on the other, particularly if the second partner feels uncomfortable with it.

A solid biblical guiding principle for all of life, including sexual behavior, is to ask the question, "Does it edify?" That's the point Paul made to the believers in the city of Corinth. "'Everything is permissible'—but not everything is beneficial. 'Everything is permissible'—but not everything is constructive. Nobody should seek his own good, but the good of others" (1 Cor. 10:23-24). Paul's point is that although Christian believers are not bound under the law, and therefore "everything is permissible," not everything is helpful or constructive. Another word for "constructive" is *edifying*. To *edify* means "to build up" something or to "strengthen" it.

When we evaluate the rightness or wrongness of actions or behavior, we need to ask ourselves if that behavior will edify—build up—ourselves or someone else, or if it will tear down. The question is not what we can get away with, but what is healthy and edifying. When it is all said and done, are we edified spiritually? Have we been built up and strengthened in our relationship with the Lord or with our spouse, or have we been weakened? Do we come away encouraged or discouraged, confident or filled with a sense of guilt or shame? Is our conscience clean?

 The question is not what we can get away with, but what is healthy and edifying.

The measure of whether or not a sexual behavior is appropriate for us is whether or not it edifies us. Whatever we can do and be edified afterwards is lawful and appropriate. If it does not edify, it is inappropriate. God has provided in His Word solid principles to guide our behavior, and those principles are always a reliable standard.

PRINCIPLES

1. Sex is not love.

2. Sex is not spiritual.

3. Sex is 100 percent physical and chemical.

4. Sex is an appetite.

5. Sex is for procreation.

6. Sex is for recreation and release.

7. Sex is for communication.

8. Sexual fulfillment and happiness in marriage depend on an open, loving, accepting, and affirming environment in which each spouse feels comfortable making his or her needs and desires known to the other.

8. A solid biblical guiding principle for all of life, including sexual behavior, is to ask the question, "Does it edify?"

CHAPTER SEVEN

Family Planning

*I*n recent years, no matter where I travel in different parts of the world to meet with government officials and religious leaders alike, when I ask them what the number one problem is in their society, I routinely get the same answer: the condition of the family. I hear this in the Caribbean, in South America, in the United States, in Israel—everywhere I go. The deterioration of the family is a universal problem.

It should come as no surprise to us that the institution of the family is under such attack from the enemy. Destruction of the family will lead to the breakdown of civilization. The family is the first and most basic unit of human society. Families are the building blocks with which every society and culture is constructed. In essence, the family is the prototype of society. A prototype is the first of its kind and demonstrates the basic characteristics of all the "models" that follow. In other words, the condition of society reflects the condition of the family. Just as a building is only as strong as the materials used to construct it, so any society is only as strong as its families.

God invented the family right at the very beginning, and it is still His ideal institution for establishing human society. Therefore, the cure for all of the social, psychological, emotional, spiritual, and civic problems that we face in our communities lies in rediscovering, restoring, and rebuilding the family.

The condition of society reflects the condition of the family.

Everything that exists has a purpose. As Creator, God had a specific purpose in mind for everything He made. This is as true for the family as for anything else. Humanity's first family was established when God made Eve from a portion of Adam's side and presented her to him (see Gen. 2:21-24). The Book of Genesis is specific regarding God's purpose for the family: "So God created man in His own image, in the image of God He created him; *male and female He created them.* God blessed them and said to them, '*Be fruitful and increase in number*; fill the earth and subdue it. Rule over the fish of the sea and the birds of the air and over every living creature that moves on the ground'" (Gen. 1:27-28 emphasis added). God's desire was to fill the earth with human beings made in His image, and the family was the avenue He chose for accomplishing it.

Another clue to God's purpose for the family is found in the Book of Malachi, the last book in the Old Testament. The people of God were upset because He seemed to no longer answer their prayers. Malachi explained why:

Another thing you do: You flood the Lord's altar with tears. You weep and wail because He no longer pays attention to your offerings or accepts them with pleasure from your hands. You ask, "Why?" It is because the Lord is acting as the witness between you and the wife of your youth, because you have broken faith with her, though she is your partner, the wife of your marriage covenant. **Has not the Lord made them one?** *In flesh and spirit they are His.* **And why one? Because He was seeking godly offspring.** *So guard yourself in your spirit, and do not break faith with the wife of your youth* (Malachi 2:13-15 emphasis added).

Children are dear to God's heart. The growth and perpetuation of human society both depend on children. From the beginning God established a firm foundation upon which to build society. Stage one was the creation of man—male and female. Stage two was marriage, a spiritual union in which two individual humans are fused into one and that is consummated physically through the act of sexual intercourse. Marriage leads naturally to stage three—a family unit consisting of a father, a mother, and one or more children. This is the traditional definition of the word *family*. Although single-parent households and unmarried individuals living alone certainly qualify as families in a broader sense, the traditional understanding is more significant when we are talking about perpetuating human society and "filling the earth" with people.

A husband and wife together build a marriage. Marriage establishes a family. Children are born, grow to maturity, and establish their own families. Multiplication of families creates communities; multiplication of communities gives rise to societies; and multiplication of societies results in nations.

If there is any command of God that mankind has faithfully obeyed, it is the command to "be fruitful and increase in number." We humans have followed that instruction so diligently that in the twenty-first century the global population has reached the danger point, and millions live with the daily threat of malnutrition and starvation. In the face of this crisis, now more than ever before, conscientious people of God have a responsibility to give careful consideration to the need for deliberate family planning.

To Beget or Not to Beget

Depending on their culture or how they were brought up, many believers are uncomfortable talking about family planning. Some are confused on the subject because of inadequate or inaccurate teaching, while others have an uneasy feeling that there is something sinful about trying to "plan" such an intimate and "holy" undertaking as having children. This being the case, it is important to understand what family planning means and what it does not mean.

Simply stated, family planning involves making deliberate decisions *in advance* to avoid unwanted pregnancies and to limit the size of one's family to the number of children that the parents can adequately love, provide for, nurture, train, and protect. Carrying out these decisions requires specific, concrete actions aimed at *prevention*. In other words, family planning includes birth control. The most common means of birth control today are the condom, the diaphragm, and the birth control pill, all of which prevent pregnancy by preventing sperm cells from the male from fertilizing the ovum from the female. Birth control prevents the *conception* of a new human being.

Family planning focuses on prevention and *advance* control of child bearing. It has nothing to do with the *deliberate termination* of pregnancies. Therefore, abortion is *not* family planning. Neither is it birth control or health care. Abortion is immoral and a sin because it is the deliberate destruction of an existing human life. As such, it goes against the direct design and intention of God.

There was a time when large families were the norm and even necessary for survival, particularly in agriculturally based societies. Infant and child mortality rates were so high due to disease or injury that parents needed to produce many children in order to ensure that some would reach maturity to help work the farm as well as carry on the family line. In today's industrialized society and current economic realities, family planning and birth control simply make good sense. This is also true in many third-world cultures with pervasive poverty and malnutrition where population runs rampant because of ignorance and lack of access to legitimate birth control options.

Family planning focuses on prevention and **ADVANCE** *control of child bearing. It has nothing to do with the* **DELIBERATE TERMINATION** *of pregnancies.*

There are at least three questions regarding family planning that every couple need to answer together, preferably before they get married, but certainly no later than in the early months of their marriage. First, "Do we want children?" For a variety of reasons some couples opt not to have any children. Whether it is for career reasons, concern over health risks, the danger of passing on hereditary health problems, or whatever, this is a decision that each couple must make for themselves.

If a couple decides that they do want children, the second question they must answer is, "When?" This is a very important question. There are several major factors to consider in determining the timing for starting a family, such as maturity, whether one or both partners are in school, and whether a steady job and income are in place. In order to grow up healthy, children need a home environment that is stable financially, emotionally, and spiritually.

A third question a couple needs to answer with regard to children is "How many?" One of the most significant factors to consider here is the couple's financial means. Very simply, the more children a couple has, the more it will cost to raise and care for them properly. For example, a household that brings in an income of $300.00 a week cannot reasonably expect to provide for ten children. It is the parents' responsibility to determine not only how many children they want, but also how many children they can realistically support.

Raising children is a serious and important matter to God, and parents are accountable to Him for how they treat and care for their children. "If anyone does not provide for his relatives, and especially for his immediate family, he has denied the faith and is worse than an unbeliever" (1 Tim. 5:8). God is not opposed to the idea of couples having a lot of children, but He does expect and require them to love, support, and provide for those children in a responsible manner.

It is the parents' responsibility to determine not only how many children they want, but also how many children they can realistically support.

Birth control can be a blessing, especially for young newlyweds who need time to adjust to each other and establish their household before bringing children into the picture. For couples who desire no children or who have all the children they want, procedures are available to prevent further conception: a vasectomy for the man or a tubal ligation for the woman. All of these are blessings of technology that are invaluable for helping married couples make wise and informed decisions concerning the size of their families.

Children are a Heritage from the Lord

Married couples who decide to have children desire a good thing. The Bible is full of passages that describe the blessings related to bearing and raising children. In Old Testament times, parents who had many children were considered to be extraordinarily blessed by God. At the same time, women who were unable to bear children were thought to be under God's curse. Although we recognize today that there is no link between the size of one's family and the blessings of God, this attitude reveals just how valuable and important children were to the people of ancient times, and particularly to the Hebrews, the children of God.

Sons are a heritage from the Lord, children a reward from Him. Like arrows in the hands of a warrior are sons born in one's youth. Blessed is the man whose quiver is full of them. They will not be put to shame when they contend with their enemies in the gate (Psalm 127:3-5).

As I stated in Chapter Six, the Hebrew word for "sons" in verses 3 and 4 also can be translated as "children." The word *children* in verse 3 is a translation of two Hebrew words that literally mean "fruit of the womb." Children are fruit, the product of their parents' fruitfulness. Thus, married couples who have children fulfill one of God's purposes for marriage: "Be fruitful and increase in number" (Gen 1:28a).

 Married couples who decide to have children desire a good thing.

Verse 4 in Psalm 127 compares children to arrows in a warrior's hand, and verse 5 states that a man whose "quiver" is full of children is blessed. Arrows are not made to stay in the quiver, however, but to be shot from a bow at the target. As long as an arrow rests in the quiver it cannot fulfill the purpose for which it was made. The same is true with children. Children rest for a time in the "quiver" of their home and family while they learn and grow to maturity, but the day eventually comes when they need to be released into the world. Only then can they fulfill the purpose and unleash the full potential that God has implanted in them. It is the role of the parents to prepare their children to leave the quiver.

God is looking for godly offspring (see Mal. 2:15), and godly offspring come about best through godly parents. His goal is for His children to have His nature and His character—to be like Him. The best way to become like God is to imitate Him. Only believers and followers of Christ can truly become like God because to do so requires the indwelling presence of the Holy Spirit. Writing to the body of believers in Ephesus, Paul had this to say: "Be imitators of God, therefore, as dearly loved children and live a life of love, just as Christ loved us and gave Himself up for us as a fragrant offering and sacrifice to God" (Eph. 5:1-2).

Jesus Christ Himself is our model. As Jesus is toward us, so we should be toward our children. One of the goals of parenting is to raise children who act like their parents, who share similar beliefs and values. Example is the greatest teacher of all, and children learn more from the lifestyle modeled by their parents than from anything their parents say. Actions really do speak louder than words.

Proverbs 20:11 says, "Even a child is known by his actions, by whether his conduct is pure and right." Where do children learn pure and right conduct if not from their parents? For better or for worse, the attitudes and behavior of children reflect the parenting they have received. In the vast majority of cases, behavioral problems in children and adolescents can be traced back to poor parental modeling.

 As Jesus is toward us, so we should be toward our children.

Good parenting is no accident. It cannot be done passively or from a distance, either physically or emotionally. Effective parenting is focused, intentional, and deliberate. Parents must *plan* for success, and godly offspring is the goal. If our children grow up sharing our moral, ethical, and spiritual values, we have succeeded as parents. If they learn to love, worship, follow and serve the Lord, we have succeeded as parents.

Who of us would not take the greatest care to protect and preserve a treasure in our possession? There is no greater treasure on earth than our children. They are a heritage from God, and as godly parents we have a responsibility and an obligation under God to treat them as such. Our goal is to produce godly offspring who will glorify and honor their heavenly Father.

Foundational Principles of Parenting

In a very real sense God was the first parent because He produced "children" designed to be like Himself. This is revealed in the very first statement He made regarding mankind as recorded in the Book of Genesis. "Then God said, 'Let us make man in our image, in our likeness...'" (Gen. 1:26a).

Contained in this verse are three foundational principles of parenting, wrapped up in the two words *image* and *likeness*. An image is a direct resemblance of an original and represents its nature or character. The word *likeness* means to look like, act like, and be like someone or something else.

God created humans to be a direct resemblance of Him; they would live, behave, and be like Him in every essential way. This truth carries clear implications for parents.

Foundational Principle #1: *Parenting should reproduce the nature of the parent in the child.* God is holy, and He created man to be holy. Sin corrupted man's holiness and distorted the divine image in him. Ever since, God's purpose and intent have been to restore man to his original holy nature. That is the very reason He sent His Son, Jesus Christ, to live in the flesh. By His life, Jesus showed us what God is like and, by His death for our sins, made it possible for His image and holiness to be fully restored in us.

By the same token, if we as parents desire godly children, we must live godly lives as an example. God is holy and righteous by nature, and He wants children who exhibit the same nature. Parenting should reproduce the nature of the parent in the child. Only the Spirit of God can reproduce the nature of God, whether in us or in our children. That is why we must depend completely on the Lord and walk closely with Him as we seek to parent our children wisely and effectively.

 If we as parents desire godly children, we must live godly lives as an example.

Foundational Principle #2: *Parenting should reproduce the character of the parent in the child.* Nature and character are very closely related. Our character is determined by the nature that controls us. It reveals who we *really* are, regardless of how we present ourselves to others. Closely akin to our reputation, character refers to our moral excellence and firmness (or lack thereof) and touches on the mental and ethical traits that mark us as individuals. Character is the person we are when no one else is around.

From a parenting point of view, this is very important. One way to measure our effectiveness as parents is by how our children act in our absence. What do they say and do when we are not around to approve or disapprove or to commend or correct? Whether we like it or not, our children very likely will become like us. It's a part of nature—children turn out like their parents. If we want to produce children of high character, we must be parents of high character.

 Character is the person we are when no one else is around.

Foundational Principle #3: *Parenting should reproduce the behavior of the parent in the child.* Nature determines character, and character determines behavior. When parents focus on their children's behavior alone, they are doomed ultimately to failure and frustration because behavior is linked to character.

As with character, parents who desire good behavior *from* their children must model good behavior *for* their children.

The old "do as I say, not as I do" approach, besides being hypocritical, simply will not work. Children can see right through hypocrisy, and they quickly lose respect for people who say one thing and do another.

If we are good and godly parents, our children will have a good and godly nature. If we are upright in all our dealings, our children will develop strong character. If we behave ourselves as parents, our children will learn to behave themselves.

We must always look not just to our children, but to *their* children as well. The final test for our effectiveness as parents is how our grandchildren turn out. If we have done our job, our children will internalize our nature, character, and behavior and pass them on to their own children. In this way, righteousness can be passed from generation to generation. This fulfills God's plan, for He is looking for godly offspring.

The final test for our effectiveness as parents is how our grandchildren turn out.

Parental Mandates

Parenting is a great joy, but it is also a great responsibility. God has made clear in His Word, the Bible, what He requires and expects of parents and holds them accountable for. His mandate is simple: Parents, train your children.

Train a child in the way he should go, and when he is old he will not turn from it (Proverbs 22:6).

The rod of correction imparts wisdom, but a child left to himself disgraces his mother (Proverbs 29:15).

He who spares the rod hates his son, but he who loves him is careful to discipline him (Proverbs 13:24).

Discipline your son, for in that there is hope; do not be a willing party to his death (Proverbs 19:18).

These commandments that I give you today are to be upon your hearts. Impress them on your children. Talk about them when you sit at home and when you walk along the road, when you lie down and when you get up (Deuteronomy 6:6-7).

Proverbs 22:6 illustrates the importance of training children while they are still very young: When they are old (or grown), they "will not turn from it." Reputable studies have shown that a child's basic character is formed by the age of seven. What we fail to teach and impart to our children during their first seven years of life, they will learn later only with great difficulty, if at all. Early training establishes the foundation for later life. Even when older children and adolescents test their boundaries (as they always do), they generally return to the beliefs and values they learned in their earliest years, if those lessons were taught with integrity and consistency and by parental example.

 A child's basic character is formed by the age of seven.

Good parenting always involves training. This is so because, first of all, *children need training*. Training is not the same as counseling. Some parents try to counsel their children regardless of age. Generally speaking, the younger the child, the less effective counseling will be. Young children need to be trained to obey first and later to understand why. This is for their own protection. As they grow in reasoning and analytical skills, they are better able to understand the "why" of their training. We must be careful not to make the mistake of trying to counsel our children before they are ready.

 Good parenting always involves training.

Secondly, *children cannot train themselves*. This should go without saying, yet there are still many parents who basically let their children make all of their own decisions and generally fend for themselves, even at very early ages. Training of the children is almost non-existent. When questioned, these parents often defend their actions (or inaction) by claiming that they don't want to force their own beliefs on their children or restrict their children's freedom to choose their own path. This is sheer folly and a recipe for disaster because children have not yet developed the capacity to make wise and mature choices. They need the clear and steady guidance of adults who can show them the way. They need the training of parents.

Thirdly, *training must be intentional*. The raising and teaching of children is too important a job to be approached haphazardly or left to chance. Parents must willingly and deliberately shoulder this burden. We are the first line of defense for our children, the first and primary source for their training and example. Good or bad, right or wrong, our children will take their lead from us. Our training and example must be fair, consistent, and unified. In matters of household rules, routine, and discipline, parents should always present a united front so that their children do not learn to play one parent against the other.

Good or bad, right or wrong, our children will take their lead from us.

Fourthly, *training focuses on the long term*. We must not expect our children to be good instantly or to learn everything the first time they are told. Training is a developmental process. Maturity does not come overnight. As parents we must always look far ahead to our children's future and to their children's future. Where training and discipline are concerned, short-term pain means long-term gain. It may break our heart to inflict the pain of discipline on our children and to see their tears, but the long-term goal of preparing them to live responsibly as adults justifies the short-term pain of disciplining them while they are young.

Finally, *failure to train is a commitment to destroy the child.* Remember Proverbs 19:18: "Discipline your son, for in that there is hope; do not be a willing party to his death." That verse tells us that our failure to discipline our children makes us a party to their destruction. If our children go wrong and mess up their lives because we did not teach them properly, then we bear the greatest burden of responsibility. We become unwitting accomplices to their destruction, in cahoots with those forces in the world that seek to destroy our children.

Be the Engine, Not the Caboose

I have one final word of counsel for parents or hope-to-be parents: *Be the engine, not the caboose.* The engine provides power for a train and determines both the direction and pace that the train will travel. Like all the other cars, the caboose follows the engine; it never leads. Wherever the engine goes the caboose goes. If the train is an analogy for the family, then the parents are the engine and the children are the caboose. Children should follow where their parents lead. Parents go ahead of their children, determining the route and speed. As long as the engine arrives safely at its destination, the rest of the train will also.

One of the big problems in many families is that the parents have allowed themselves to become the caboose. Their children have seized control of the engine and are off and running with no sense of direction or purpose, and all the parents can do is be pulled along as the "train" of their family goes careering down the track. Eventual derailment and destruction are virtually certain. Whatever else we do as parents, we must never allow our children to run the train.

The engine determines which track the train runs on. In the same way, we as parents determine where our children go and what they become by the track that we put our own lives on. Ahead of us lies a fork in the track, and we can switch our train onto one or the other. One leads to life and health and prosperity, while the other leads to death and destruction. The choice is ours: Which way will we go?

 Whatever else we do as parents, we must never allow our children to run the train.

God is seeking godly offspring. He wants us to choose life for ourselves and for our children. In the words of Moses, the "friend of God":

> *This day I call heaven and earth as witnesses against you that I have set before you life and death, blessings and curses. Now choose life, so that you and your children may live and that you may love the Lord your God, listen to His voice, and hold fast to Him. For the Lord is your life, and He will give you many years in the land He swore to give to your fathers, Abraham, Isaac and Jacob* (Deuteronomy 30:19-20).

Children need the love, guidance, training, discipline, and protection that only parents can provide. The strength and health of the next generation depend on the faithfulness and diligence of the parents of this generation. Married couples who decide to have children choose a good thing. Yes, raising children is an awesome responsibility that carries with it a sizeable portion of frustration, heartache, and stress. More than that, however, parenting is a wonderful privilege that is accompanied by great joy, deep satisfaction, and abundant hope for the future.

PRINCIPLES

1. Family planning involves making deliberate decisions in advance to avoid unwanted pregnancies and to limit the size of one's family to the number of children that the parents can adequately love, provide for, nurture, train, and protect.

2. Family planning involves answering three questions with regard to children: "Do we want children?"; "When?"; and "How many?"

3. In order to grow up healthy, children need a home environment that is stable financially, emotionally, and spiritually.

4. Example is the greatest teacher of all, and children learn more from the lifestyle modeled by their parents than from anything their parents say.

5. Effective parenting is focused, intentional, and deliberate.

6. Parenting should reproduce the nature of the parent in the child.

7. Parenting should reproduce the character of the parent in the child.

8. Parenting should reproduce the behavior of the parent in the child.

9. God's mandate is simple: Parents, train your children.

10. Parents should be the engine, not the caboose.

CHAPTER EIGHT

Living Under Agape

Marriage that lasts a lifetime must be built on a solid foundation that will not rot, erode, or wear away over time. A successful, happy, and fruitful marital relationship must be founded on principles that are permanent, not temporary; forged from things that last, not fade away.

Physical attractiveness won't do it. External beauty fades over time. Hair turns gray or white or falls out, skin wrinkles, muscles turn flabby, waistlines enlarge, teeth come out, eyesight dims, hearing diminishes. If you have built your marriage relationship on physical attraction, what will you do when the physical attributes that initially drew you together disappear?

Sex won't do it. Moods and attitudes change and evolve. With increasing age both the ability to perform sexually and the interest in sexual activity decline. In the meantime, an appetite that is 100 percent physical and chemical is insufficient by itself to nourish and sustain a relationship that is essentially spiritual in nature.

Finances won't do it. Due to economic downturns, job loss, physical disability, long-term illness, or a host of other factors, financial status can change drastically very quickly. A marriage based solely or primarily on economic factors or earning potential is a recipe for failure.

Possessions won't do it. As permanent and substantial as material things appear, they are only temporary and can fly away with the morning breeze. Just ask anyone who has suddenly lost everything in a disastrous fire or a hurricane. What's more, centering our life or marriage around the accumulation of possessions simply creates an insatiable hunger for more, a craving that can never be satisfied.

Upon what, then, can a married couple build a happy, secure, and lasting relationship? What foundation will stand the test of time as well as the storms of adversity? I hope I have made it clear throughout this book that the only sure foundation for a lifelong marriage is *agape*, the self-giving love that has its source and origin in God alone. Only that which derives from God Himself will last; everything else is transitory. Writing to the community of believers in Corinth, Paul had this to say about the lasting quality of agape:

> *Love never fails. But where there are prophecies, they will cease; where there are tongues, they will be stilled; where there is knowledge, it will pass away. For we know in part and we prophesy in part, but when perfection comes, the imperfect disappears....And now these three remain: faith, hope and love. But the greatest of these is love* (1 Corinthians 13:8-10,13).

In the end, faith, hope, and love will remain. All of these have their origin in God, and love (*agape*) is the greatest of the three. This is so because faith and hope arise from God's love and can exist only in the environment of His presence. Because God is eternal and *agape* is His very nature, His love can never fail. Prophecies, tongues, and knowledge—all the things that seem so permanent to us—will someday disappear. These things also have their origin in God, but they are by His design temporary in nature. When they have fulfilled their purpose, they will pass away. It is different with love. *Agape* is eternal; it will never pass away.

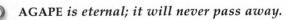 **AGAPE *is eternal; it will never pass away.***

Love Is an Ongoing Debt

In Chapter One we learned that *agape* is unconditional love—love without reason—the sacrificial, self-giving kind of love that Jesus demonstrated when He died on the cross for our sins. Love without reason means loving regardless of the loveableness of the people involved and whether or not they reciprocate in that love. *Agape* sets forth no conditions, makes no demands, and holds no expectations. It carries no guarantee except to guarantee itself.

A marriage based on *agape*, then, is a roleless relationship because spouses love each other unconditionally, sacrificially, and without fixed expectations of each other. Fueled by love, their relationship is characterized by responding to needs rather than conforming to fixed roles.

For believers, *agape* should be the guiding and motivating force behind all relationships, marriage or otherwise. Simon Peter, one of Jesus' closest friends and followers, had this to say about the unconditional, non-expectant nature of *agape*: "Above all, love each other deeply, because *love covers over a multitude of sins*" (1 Pet. 4:8 emphasis added). *Agape* does not overlook or ignore sin; it *covers over* sin, just as the blood of Jesus covers our sin to put us in a right relationship with God. In marriage, *agape* means that spouses, rather than overlook each other's faults and weaknesses, relate redemptively to each other and allow love to overcome each other's shortcomings and not allow them to become points of strife and conflict.

Love is an ongoing debt that we owe each other, a debt that should never be paid off. Paul made this clear when he wrote to the believers in Rome, "Let no debt remain outstanding, except the continuing debt to love one another, for he who loves his fellowman has fulfilled the law" (Rom. 13:8). If we get into the habit of thinking of ourselves as always owing a debt of love to our spouses, we will be less inclined to take offense when they say or do something that we do not like. The implication of Paul's words is that we are to love others *always*, regardless of their attitude or response toward us.

 If we get into the habit of thinking of ourselves as always owing a debt of love to our spouses, we will be less inclined to take offense when they say or do something that we do not like.

Love Lived Out

What then are the practical implications for married couples living under *agape*? Understanding the answer requires first of all a good working definition of *agape* in practical terms. I believe we could find no better definition than the one found in the thirteenth chapter of Paul's first letter to the believers in Corinth:

> *Love is patient, love is kind. It does not envy, it does not boast, it is not proud. It is not rude, it is not self-seeking, it is not easily angered, it keeps no record of wrongs. Love does not delight in evil but rejoices with the truth. It always protects, always trusts, always hopes, always perseveres. Love never fails* (1 Corinthians 13:4-8a).

Let's consider each of these points briefly with regard to the relationship between husbands and wives. At all times in all things we should be careful to heed Jesus' words, "Do to others as you would have them do to you" (Lk. 6:31).

Love is patient. Always remember that no one is perfect. We all have our own faults and flaws, our own particular idiosyncrasies and annoying habits or mannerisms. Everyone enters marriage with a certain amount of emotional, psychological, and spiritual baggage. Adjusting to each other's uniqueness takes time and *patience*. The King James Version often uses the word *longsuffering* for patience, which really captures the idea of what we're talking about here. Patient love makes allowances for individual differences and seeks to understand before speaking or judging. In our marriage relationships we all need healthy allowances of grace, not only that which we extend toward our spouses, but also that which they extend to us. Patient love is full of grace. Rather than finding fault, it seeks to help the other person reach his or her full potential and personhood in Christ.

 Patient love is full of grace.

Love is kind. The Greek word for "kind" in verse 4 literally means "to show oneself useful" or "to act benevolently." Kind love is always seeking after the best interests of the other person, actively looking for ways to help, comfort, encourage, strengthen, and lift up. This is where remembering the little things comes into play—a compliment, a card, a bouquet of roses. There is more involved here than just thoughtfulness, however. Kindness is active, deliberate engagement in pursuing the welfare of another. It is gentle and tender, yet firm and tough when necessary, refusing to stand idly by and allow loved ones to engage in self-destructive behavior. Sometimes the greatest act of kindness is to forcibly intervene to prevent someone we love from heading down the path to ruin. Kind love is also tough love.

 Kindness is active, deliberate engagement in pursuing the welfare of another.

Love does not envy. *Agape* is a love that rests secure in itself and its relationships. When we live under *agape*, we will be comfortable with who we are and with our status and relationships with others. We will not feel threatened by their success or envious over their happiness. On the contrary, we will actively and sincerely rejoice with them over these things. To envy means to be zealous, eager, or anxious, either for or against someone, and it is closely akin to jealousy. Secure and confident as it is, *agape* pulls the fangs out of envy and jealousy, leaving them powerless. Non-envying love means that when a wife receives a nice promotion at work, her husband won't feel threatened by or in competition with her success, but honestly rejoice with her. It means that when a husband is honored by his colleagues, his wife will sincerely take pride in his recognition and not fear that any attention is being taken away from her. Love that does not envy is love that has learned to be content, whatever the circumstances.

 AGAPE *is a love that rests secure in itself and its relationships.*

Love does not boast. Literally, to boast means to play the braggart. A braggart is someone who is always sounding his own praises or "tooting his own horn." He wants to make sure everyone knows about his gifts and accomplishments. In reality, braggarts usually accomplish little of use to anyone else because they spend all their time boasting. Love, on the other hand, is always too busy *doing* good to spend time talking about it. Those who live under *agape* have no need or drive to boast because they find their fulfillment and purpose not in the praise and recognition of men but in the opportunity to serve the needs of others in the name of Christ. If we feel a need to boast about or broadcast our love, that is a sure sign that no love is present. *Agape* neither needs nor seeks fanfare. True love reveals itself by its actions, and when it is present, everyone knows it.

Love is always too busy DOING *good to spend time talking about it.*

Love is not proud. Pride is the great sin of mankind, the sin of Adam and Eve that brought their downfall in Eden. The Greek word literally refers to a pair of bellows pumped up with air. A proud person is arrogant, with an inflated ego that is puffed up in vain self-confidence, smugly reliant on his own powers, talents, and knowledge. Love is the exact opposite: humble, gentle, never forceful. Families who live under *agape* treat each other always with dignity, honor, and respect because they know that they are equally dependent upon God for all things and equally indebted to Him for their forgiveness and righteous standing with Him through Christ. Pride always focuses on the self; *agape* never does, focusing instead on God and on other people. *Agape* destroys pride because where love fills all, there is no room for pride.

 AGAPE *destroys pride because where love fills all, there is no room for pride.*

Love is not rude. In many segments of modern society, rudeness seems commonplace, even expected. Nonetheless, polite behavior has never gone out of style. Good manners are always appropriate. Rudeness means to act unbecomingly, improperly, or indecently, and in a manner deserving of reproach. Love seeks always to act properly and becomingly in every circumstance and relationship of life. This means showing due honor and respect for the place and opinions of others, whether higher or lower in rank. All persons, regardless of status, are worthy of respect and decency. People living under *agape* are careful to maintain proper respect and behavior in all the relationships of life: husband, wife, parent, child, brother, sister, son, or daughter. Love that is not rude also acts to prevent anything that would violate decency.

Good manners are always appropriate.

Love is not self-seeking. This is another way of defining a roleless love—love without conditions or expectations. *Agape* has no ulterior or selfish motives; it is unconditional. Conditional love sets limits; *agape* sets none. This kind of love seeks the welfare of others even at the cost of self-denial and personal sacrifice. Living under *agape* means that we are not concerned primarily with seeking our own happiness, but the happiness of others, and that we will not pursue our happiness at the expense of others. People who live under *agape* live for the purpose of doing good, just as Jesus did (see Acts 10:38).

People who live under AGAPE live for the purpose of doing good, just as Jesus did.

Love is not easily angered. This means that it takes a lot to provoke us. We do not rise to the bait and let anger overcome us. The Greek word carries the idea of irritation or sharpness of spirit. Agape, although it is not soft or gullible, also has no "rough edges." If we are ruled by agape, we will not be prone to violent anger or provocation, always keeping our temper in check. We will not be quick to judge or be hasty in drawing conclusions, but give others the benefit of the doubt. We will not "fly off the handle" or "go off half-cocked" whenever any little thing does not suit us. Instead, we keep in mind the words of James, Jesus' half-brother: "Everyone should be quick to listen, slow to speak and slow to become angry, for man's anger does not bring about the righteous life that God desires" (Jas. 1:19b-20).

Love keeps no record of wrongs. Two ideas are in mind here. First, love does not "keep inventory" of wrongs, hurts, insults, or offenses with a view to returning the same in kind. In other words, love has no interest in "getting even." The desire for revenge is one of the most destructive impulses in the entire realm of human relationships. People guided by *agape* will not keep bringing up past wrongs to throw in the face of the offender. The second idea is that *agape* always imputes the purest and highest motives to the actions of others. This does not mean being gullible or a pushover, but it does mean looking for and thinking the best about every person. It means neither receiving nor passing on gossip or hurtful information about another person. *Agape* never plays the "blame game" and holds the highest opinion of others until and unless clear evidence indicates otherwise.

> *Love does not "keep inventory" of wrongs, hurts, insults, or offenses with a view to returning the same in kind.*

Love does not delight in evil. The psalmist wrote, "Blessed is the man who does not walk in the counsel of the wicked or stand in the way of sinners or sit in the seat of mockers" (Ps. 1:1). That is the thought that is in mind here. Not only does *agape* refuse to associate itself in any way with wickedness and evil, but it also mourns their presence in the affairs and lives of men. If we are under the rule of *agape*, we will find no pleasure in sin, either our own or anyone else's. News of the misfortune of others, even of enemies, will sadden us because *agape* desires the best for everyone, and especially the repentance and salvation of those who are alienated from God.

> *If we are under the rule of agape, we will find no pleasure in sin, either our own or anyone else's.*

Love rejoices with the truth. Psalm 1 continues describing the "blessed" man: "But his delight is in the law of the Lord, and on His law he meditates day and night" (Ps. 1:2). There is no greater truth than the Word of God, and those who live under *agape* will take genuine delight in it. We will read it, study it, discuss it, share it, teach it to our children, and proclaim it to a dark and dying world. Rejoicing with the truth also means being genuinely happy with the honest and honorable success of others, even people who disagree with us or with whom we have trouble getting along. It means celebrating when justice prevails and injustice is overturned. Rejoicing with the truth means being happy when people come out of restrictive, self-limiting ignorance into the light of knowledge. *Agape* is active rejoicing that gets personally involved in serving and working for the truth.

Love always protects. The Greek word for "protects" literally means "to cover," as with a roof, and "to hide or conceal." In this sense, then, *agape* is always careful to hide the faults or failings of others rather than broadcast them to the world. With regard to marriage and the family, this means that a husband "covers" his wife, and both of them cover and protect their children, depending all the while on the protecting and covering *agape* of God over their lives, their circumstances, and their welfare. *Agape* is the shield or barrier that insulates a family from the harsh onslaughts of life and the arid, desiccating values of a godless world.

Love always trusts. This is true, first of all, with regard to God. Since *agape* has its source in God alone, its very life is wrapped up in Him alone. If we are guided by *agape*, we will trust the Lord in all things and will look to Him for wisdom, leadership, and discernment in every affair of life, whether at home, on the job, or elsewhere. Trust in God will permeate our conversation as well as every relationship with both family and friends. In addition, love that always trusts means having faith in other people, not to the point of gullibility, but believing the best of them unless there is irrefutable evidence to the contrary. In this sense, it is similar to the quality of keeping no record of wrongs. *Agape* delights in and assumes the virtue and good feeling of others.

Love always hopes. What is meant here is not the dreamy, wishful thinking type of hope that the world understands. *Agape* hope—biblical hope—is grounded solidly in accomplished fact and the promises of God. Because of this, if we are living under *agape*, we can have a confident and assured expectancy that our lives will turn out well. We are in the capable hands of a loving Father who promised us: "For I know the plans I have for you...plans to prosper you and not to harm you, plans to give you hope and a future" (Jer. 29:11). *Agape* always sees the bright side of things in both the physical and spiritual realms, not through denial that refuses to acknowledge pain, sorrow, and hardship, but through an optimism that refuses to despair because it is grounded in the unfailing nature and promises of God.

> **AGAPE** *hope—biblical hope—is grounded solidly in accomplished fact and the promises of God.*

Love always perseveres. When all else fails (or seems to), love never gives up. It hangs on to the end. Loving parents never give up on their children, never stop loving them, never stop praying for them, no matter how rebellious and wayward they may be. God is eternal, and since agape has its source in Him, it too is eternal. Therefore, by nature and definition, agape always perseveres. *Agape* bears up under persecution, slander, hardship, abuse, false accusations, ingratitude—anything. The persevering quality of *agape* is what Jesus displayed when He prayed from the cross for His enemies and executioners: "Father, forgive them, for they do not know what they are doing" (Lk. 23:34.)

Love never fails. This statement sums up all that has gone before. The word *fails* here is used in the sense of something giving way, falling off, or ceasing to exist. Love is eternal. Prophecies, tongues, and knowledge will someday pass away but agape will never fail. This world we live in, as well as the entire physical universe, will eventually disappear, but *agape* will never fail. *Agape* is a little bit of Heaven on earth right now, and it will remain to characterize life for all of God's people in the new Heaven and new earth that are to come. Though all else may pass away, love will remain. *Agape* never fails.

ꝏ

Learning to live under *agape* is the primary key to understanding love that lasts a lifetime. Every married couple faces the question, "Okay, we're married, now what?" Modern society offers them many different options, a multiplicity of voices that offer counsel and advice. The world has a lot to say about love—good and bad, right and wrong—but no one understands love the way God does, because God *is* love (see 1 Jn. 4:16). If we want to understand love, we need to go to the source. If we want to grow and live a successful, lifelong marriage, we need to consult the manufacturer.

Marriage is an adventurous journey, and every traveler on that road needs a reliable Guide and a trustworthy handbook. Whether you are newlyweds just starting out on your journey together or experienced veterans seeking to enrich and refresh yourselves along the way, commit your lives and your marriage to the Lord. Live for Him and follow His Word, and He will bless your journey, bring you success, and fill you with joy and contentment along the way. Consider the words of the wise man:

> *Trust in the Lord with all your heart and lean not on your own understanding; in all your ways acknowledge Him, and He will make your paths straight* (Proverbs 3:5-6).

PRINCIPLES

⊗

1. The only sure foundation for a lifelong marriage is *agape*, the self-giving love that has its source and origin in God alone.

2. Love is an ongoing debt that we owe each other, a debt that should never be paid off.

3. *Agape* is patient.

4. **Agape** is kind.

5. *Agape* does not envy.

6. *Agape* does not boast.

7. *Agape* is not proud.

8. *Agape* is not rude.

9. *Agape* is not self-seeking.

10. *Agape* is not easily angered.

11. *Agape* keeps no record of wrongs.

12. *Agape* does not delight in evil.

13. *Agape* rejoices with the truth.

14. *Agape* always protects.

15. *Agape* always trusts.

16. *Agape* always hopes.

17. *Agape* always perseveres.

18. *Agape* never fails.

Understanding Love series
by Dr. Myles Munroe

━━━ UNDERSTANDING LOVE: MARRIAGE STILL A GREAT IDEA

In this frank, honest, and insightful book, Dr. Myles Munroe cuts through the fog of ignorance and misinformation to illuminate marriage as God designed it: a pure and holy institution in which a man and a woman enter into a commitment to become "one flesh" as equal partners in a lifelong union of friendship and companionship. This timely book will help you and your spouse build a happier and stronger marriage or, if you are single and preparing for marriage, help you and your betrothed start off on the right foot.
ISBN 0-7684-2154-3

━━━ UNDERSTANDING LOVE FOR A LIFETIME

Thoroughly biblical and eminently practical, *Understanding Love for a Lifetime* addresses such critical marital issues as communication, financial management, developing true intimacy, and family planning and parenting. *Understanding Love for a Lifetime* is a simple and refreshingly lucid guide that will help newlywed or soon-to-be-wed couples chart their way to marital success and avoid the "reefs" that could cause their marriage to flounder.
ISBN 0-7684-2156-X

━━━ UNDERSTANDING LOVE AND THE SECRETS OF THE HEART

Dr. Munroe examines love in general from many different angles with the purpose of bringing the reader to an understanding of biblical love as the central foundation for all relationships in life, both human and divine. *Understanding Love and the Secrets of the Heart* provides a solid foundation of knowledge and understanding for anyone involved in or anticipating a serious relationship.
ISBN 0-7684-2155-1

Available at your local Christian bookstore.

**For more information and sample chapters,
visit www.destinyimage.com**

Additional copies of this book and other
book titles from DESTINY IMAGE are
available at your local bookstore.

For a complete list of our titles,
visit us at www.destinyimage.com
Send a request for a catalog to:

Destiny Image® Publishers, Inc.
P.O. Box 310
Shippensburg, PA 17257-0310

*"Speaking to the Purposes of God for This
Generation and for the Generations to Come"*